PRAISE FOR AVIVE LA VIE

Avive la Vie—An Adventure in Belonging explores the dynamics of human connection, uncovering a key to healthy relationships. JF Benoist's emphasis on fostering a genuine sense of belonging mirrors one of the core principles of psychological flexibility in Acceptance and Commitment Therapy and of the deeper clinical traditions. In this uplifting narrative, Benoist weaves together personal stories and practical guidance to demonstrate how our False Belonging Habits—patterns of striving for approval or suppressing emotions to gain acceptance—can hinder true connection. The characters in the book reflect the universal challenge of reconnecting with the inherent value and love we all carry within. Benoist's invitation to the reader to explore and challenge our patterns of behavior asks us to take a transformative journey through the book itself. It is a warm and engaging resource for anyone seeking a deeper understanding of themselves and a more meaningful connection with others.

> **—Steven C. Hayes, PhD, Originator of Acceptance and Commitment Therapy and Foundation Professor Emeritus of Psychology, University of Nevada, Reno**

An engaging, not-to-be-missed treasure! *Avive la Vie* takes the reader on a journey into the heart of what it takes to know, accept, and attune to oneself. In a deftly crafted story, JF Benoist's relatable characters illuminate the struggles we face—and the shifts we can make—to evolve toward our better selves. Masterfully focusing on core concepts of self-attunement, resilience, and personal growth, this thought-provoking book helps us notice and break free from the false beliefs that feed doubt, repression, and the habits that keep us stuck. A gentle, masterful guide to finding the self, freeing the self, and loving the self … a journey for us all!

—Carla Marie Manly, PhD, Clinical Psychologist,
Author of ***The Joy of Imperfect Love: The Art of***
Creating Healthy, Securely Attached Relationships

One of those engaging narratives that brings readers into the story in ways that expand understanding and shift perspectives. It shows the power of adopting a 'connection first' way of living and helps people see—in safe, relatable ways—how to shed past patterns and embrace essential human birthrights: inherent worth, natural resilience, and self-love.

—Ellen Petry Leanse, Neuroscience Educator,
Bestselling Author of ***The Happiness Hack***

If you're looking for a path out of the loneliness epidemic, here you go! *Avive la Vie* shows a simple way to shift ourselves from loneliness and social anxiety into connection and belonging. It's all right here: inspiring stories, step-by-step guidance, and an invitation to join with other readers in practicing connection. This story literally leaps off the page and into a real-life social adventure. *Belonging* is your birthright; here's how to make it happen.

—David Cates, Author of ***Unconditional Money:***
A Magical Journey into the Heart of Abundance

AVIVE LA VIE

(Ah-veev lah Vee)

An Adventure in Belonging

JF Benoist

Published by Pakalana Publishing
ISBN: 979-8-9882868-1-3

Editor: Brooke Carey and Danielle Anderson
Contributing Editors: David Cates, Joyce Marvel-Benoist
Typeset: Elite Authors
Book Cover Design: Vanessa Mendozzi

Disclaimer: Jean-Francois (J.F.) Benoist is the founder of
the Avive la Vie movement who teaches methods of self-reflection
but does not prescribe or diagnose in any way. The materials and
services offered by Benoist are intended to encourage and to teach
skills that support positive attitudinal and relational change.

This book is not intended to replace or simulate medical advice
of any kind. The contents of this book are intended to be used as an
adjunct to a rational and responsible healthcare program prescribed by
a healthcare practitioner. The author and publisher are in no way liable
for any use or misuse of this material.

A Note on Privacy
Confidentiality and discretion are the highest priorities in J.F. Benoist's
work. Because of this, Benoist has taken real life types of events to
create simulated stories and characters in this book. Any resemblance
to any specific person or persons is purely coincidental.

TABLE OF CONTENTS

INTRODUCTION

THE QUEST FOR BELONGING

C orrection: wasn't that the main method of teaching that our parents, teachers, and community used on us? *Don't put a fork in the electrical socket. Don't run with scissors. Don't pull on the cat's tail.*

We had to learn to not touch a hot stove so we didn't burn ourselves. But over time, there was a shift away from correcting us for our own safety toward correcting us so we'd be acceptable members of society. *Don't play in muddy puddles, you'll look sloppy. Don't put your elbows on the table, that's rude. Don't cry in public, it makes you look weak.*

This could be done in more subtle ways, too, of course. *You're not going to wear that to school, are you? Why can't you be more like your brother and get "A"s?*

This is what we experienced throughout our childhood years: learning the "proper" way to navigate the world and feeling the consequences of what happened when we didn't follow cultural norms. If we wanted to belong in society, we had to constantly improve or change ourselves in some way.

But how does that *feel?* Do you feel inspired after comparing yourself to your colleagues? Do you feel motivated when you look in the mirror and dissect all the things you think are wrong with you?

These corrections, the very things our caregivers were trying to use to help us succeed, started becoming counterproductive. Rather than building confidence in our abilities to be a part of our community, they strip us of our self-certainty. At some level, many of us learned to believe that we can't belong just the way we are. We think we have to play a part or fulfill this preconceived role of who we should be.

This way of thinking leads us to believe that we aren't good enough, lovable enough, valuable enough unless we tick every box we think the world expects us to. As adults, these constant comparisons and corrections have led to a cycle that holds many of us back today—a pattern of correcting ourselves called False Belonging Habits. These corrective thoughts pop up in times of stress, urging us to change our behavior in order to appease the people around us.

> *If I impress them with my work, they'll think I'm smart—and I'll belong.*
> *If I prioritize everyone else over myself, they'll value my care—and I'll belong.*
> *If I agree with them, they'll like me—and I'll belong.*

These False Belonging Habits offer the promise of belonging sometime in the future, so long as we mold ourselves into the person we think others want us to be. Yet we actually end up feeling even more disconnected from ourselves and others in our present reality.

That's because true belonging doesn't have prerequisites. It doesn't require us to prove anything. We don't have to fix, change, or correct ourselves to be completely and utterly valuable, loveable, and deserving of our place in the world.

The truth is that each and every one of us already belongs—and our False Belonging Habits can offer insight and wisdom on our quest to experience true belonging.

PUTTING THE FOCUS ON CONNECTION

Before we can move forward, we have to once again look to our past. All that time, when your parents or teachers or grandparents were correcting you, what took a back seat?

Connection.

Think about it. When you came home with a bad grade on your report card, did your mom or dad focus on how you were feeling? Or ask if there was a reason behind the bad mark?

Or, were they only focused on the fact that you did poorly?

Time and time again, when our elders thought they were preparing us for the "real world," they dismissed our experience, emotions, and connection. Here lies the key to breaking out of our False Belonging Habits: restoring a genuine, unfiltered connection to our core selves.

You may be surprised to find that human beings at their core all look pretty similar. We're not talking about philosophies or beliefs; we're referring to internal qualities that we all share: courage, resilience, love, and value. In the correction-based world we live in, few of us stay fully connected to these qualities. What would our lives look like if we did?

To show you the power of a connection-first lifestyle, this book follows the stories of seven different people—one who exemplifies belonging (Rowan) and a crew of six who face the same everyday struggles you do: relationship issues, grief, self-doubt, lack of fulfillment in work. As you get to know "the Crew," you'll notice that they all attempt to belong in a different way, and you'll get a chance to assess if you subscribe to the same False Belonging Habit that they do. We each have our own unique blend of Habits, so don't be surprised if you identify with more than one. Once we can recognize our primary Habits, we can observe them with acceptance, curiosity, and insight. Judging ourselves has never really helped, so we are exploring a new way to invite change with a compassionate, inquisitive approach.

As the stories progress, you'll also get to see how the Crew learn to embrace connection in their life and find a sense of belonging. This is an adventure—an exploration—so remaining curious and open-minded are the best ways to move forward on this journey.

After you've followed the Crew's journeys and identified your own top False Belonging Habit(s), then we'll get into the practical tools of how to apply this newfound knowledge to your life. You'll learn skills to begin to navigate your unique Habits so you can fully embrace a connection-first way of living. We'll give examples of how to strengthen your relationship with your courage, resilience, innate value, and innate love. You can eventually be connected to them without even thinking about it.

Experiencing a sense of true belonging is in our nature. Once you learn the building blocks, you can effortlessly embody this way of living with belonging at your core. And when you're aligned with your core love and value, you will have the confidence and composure to take on whatever challenges life throws at you.

PART 1
MEET ROWAN AND
THE CREW

CHAPTER 1

CORRECTION VERSUS CONNECTION

Many years ago

Kenta shivered as he walked to the pool at the campground. Though only ten, he had been competitively swimming for three years; he'd always been a good swimmer, and he loved being in the water, so his parents had signed him up for the local junior team the day he was old enough. The family had just arrived to spend spring break at a cabin, and Kenta needed to swim at least twice a day to keep in shape for next week's big meet.

Kenta pulled his towel tighter around his shoulders, trying to shield himself from the chilly morning air. This April was far colder than anyone expected, and Kenta wasn't particularly excited to hop into the water. But he had to practice; he couldn't let his parents down.

As he reached the gate of the pool, he found it padlocked. He pulled, but the lock wouldn't budge. Kenta's stomach dropped.

What was he going to do? Knots formed in Kenta's stomach, twisting and tightening as he thought about missing a whole week of practice.

But then, something caught his eye.

The lake.

Kenta started walking toward it. Even though it had snowed up in the mountains last night, he couldn't see any ice, which was a good sign. It was a body of water... why couldn't he just practice there instead?

Reaching the dock, Kenta draped his towel on a post and put on his swim cap. He dipped a foot in the water.

Yowza! That was cold. Very, very cold.

Kenta took a deep breath. He'd been in cold pools before. His dad always told him that it was just mind over matter. He'd get used to it if he just got in.

Glancing back at his family's cabin in the distance, Kenta saw the sliding glass door open. His dad stepped outside, holding a cup of coffee. Kenta waved until he got his dad's attention. His dad set down his coffee mug and waved back—with two arms, strangely enough. Crossing them in front of each other.

Kenta turned back toward the lake and decided it was now or never. He took a deep inhale, then plunged in.

When Kenta popped his head back up, he was a little light-headed. This was colder than any water he'd ever experienced. But like his dad said, if he just pushed through the pain, he'd get used to it.

He decided to start with freestyle to get his muscles warmed up. He set out for the middle of the lake, one stroke after another. But for some reason, it felt like his arms were lagging. He was trying to go faster—to get up to race pace—but his arms just wouldn't move any quicker.

During one stroke, as his ear came up to the air, Kenta thought he heard someone shouting. He stopped swimming and paddled in place. He looked back at the dock and saw his parents frantically waving their arms. "Come back!" they yelled. Seeing them so nervous instantly made Kenta nervous.

He raised his arm up to signal he was okay and noticed his hand had turned an unfamiliar shade of purple. His heart started racing even faster than it had been.

He needed to get back to the shore. Now.

He started swimming as hard as he could back toward his parents, but he felt like he was swimming through a lake of syrup. There was so much resistance. His arms and legs felt so heavy. He heard his parents shout for him to hurry, but he *was* hurrying. He was doing the best he could.

The pain he had done his best to ignore was excruciating now. It felt like tiny pinpricks were stabbing every inch of his body. He wanted to stop. He desperately wanted to stop. But he knew he couldn't.

Finally, with one last push, his arms reached the rickety ladder of the dock. He tried to climb it, but his arms could barely grasp the wood. His dad reached down and hoisted Kenta onto the dock. Instantly, his mother wrapped his towel around him and held him. An enormous feeling of relief washed over his body.

"Kenta!" his mother said sharply. "What were you thinking? This lake is freezing!" She was rubbing the towel so hard that the fibers burned Kenta's skin.

"His lips are blue. We need to get him to a hospital," his dad said, picking up his son and rushing to the car.

"I just don't know why you would have ever done that. That was so dangerous, Kenta," his mother said on the way to the car.

"That was stupid. Plain stupid," his dad grumbled, holding tightly onto his son.

"I'm... sorry..." Kenta whispered, his teeth chattering. That feeling of relief faded away, quickly replaced by embarrassment and regret.

Kenta's mom opened the back car door, and his father laid him on the seat. Kenta's mom grabbed a blanket and threw it over Kenta.

They sped off.

Resilience is an essential aspect of adulthood. The ability to pick ourselves up after we fall—and try again—is vital to being a confident person.

When we're young, our connection to our resilience is still developing, and our parents and caregivers can either encourage or erode that strength in us. Unfortunately, many parents end up unknowingly weakening their child's sense of resilience by prioritizing *correcting* their behavior. This myth that correction is what children need most has been passed down for generations, becoming an unconscious reflex for parents and caregivers. We assume that children learn from correction and will be smarter in the future. Yet, when a parent reprimands a child for their mistake, the focus becomes centered on the error rather than the warmth and safety of connection. The strength of this young person, who is trying to navigate the challenges of the world and build a strong sense of belonging, goes unacknowledged. Even more, the child's self-critic begins to build. They learn that every time they make a mistake, they need to criticize themselves for it—slowly chipping away at their confidence.

But there is another way to respond after a mistake. As adults, we often don't trust that children can quickly identify the difference between right and wrong. While we can guide our children by teaching them discernment, like how to know when water is too cold to swim in, we don't need to hammer home that they've made a poor decision. Because when a child hears us repeating that message, they're not thinking, "I'll make sure not to swim in cold water again." Instead, they're thinking about how stupid or careless or naïve they were, and their confidence in themselves tanks.

By focusing on the connection between the adult and child in the moment, the child isn't as likely to experience shame. Instead, the child can stay connected to their strength and resilience, feeling more confident to try things in the future.

*** Rowan

Last night, Rowan had asked his mom if he could go snowboarding the next morning.

"We have to leave early for the farmer's market," she'd said, "so we won't have time. We'll go this weekend, okay?" But the snowfall was just right, and Rowan didn't want to risk missing the perfect ride. So, he got up extra early and told himself he'd get in one quick run before the day started.

Rowan tiptoed out the front door, closing it as gently as he could. He grabbed his snowboard off the porch and started making his way up the large hill just a quarter mile from his house. At eight years old, Rowan had ridden down this hill hundreds of times—but always with his mother. This was his first solo ride.

After a hike to the top, Rowan checked all his gear like his mother had shown him. Helmet strap? Locked. Gloves? Secured. Boots? Locked in.

He took a deep breath, then leaned forward. Soon, the wind was whooshing over his helmet, and he couldn't have been happier.

The next thing he knew, he was lying on the snowy ground.

Rowan's eyes opened slowly, like they'd rather stay shut. His head was pounding. As his senses came back to him, he had flashes of memory: the hidden tree stump, the collision, the pain.

He felt a wet sensation on his arm and looked over to see a bone jutting out above his wrist. Blood was pouring out. His heart started racing. He couldn't seem to catch his breath, and he started shouting for his mother. Thankfully, he heard her voice call from down the hill.

Soon, she was kneeling down next to him. Rowan could see a strange look on her face; he didn't see it often. Was she scared? But before he could think any more about it, she said, "Rowan, let's do a big yell together on three, okay? One, two, three." While Rowan could only manage a small whoop, his mother let out a howl. When she looked at him again, she was in her normal state. "Okay, that's better. I'm here, honey," she said calmly. After filling her lungs with a deep breath, she whipped off her scarf and used it as a tourniquet for Rowan's arm. As she pulled it tight, he screamed.

"It hurts!" he cried, tears forming in his eyes.

"I know, I know it hurts. This is to help it from hurting worse."

"No, it hurts too much! Take it off!"

"Rowan, I want you to look at me," his mother requested sternly.

Rowan was still hyperventilating, fixated on the growing puddle of blood on the snow. "Rowan," she repeated. "Look at me."

With uneven breaths, Rowan turned his head to look at his mother.

"I'm right here, and I'm not going anywhere. Are you here with me?"

Rowan slowly nodded.

"That's right. We got this, Ro Ro."

Rowan felt his body begin to calm. It was like someone had plucked the fear right out of him, like pulling a loose thread from a sweater. If he just kept looking at his mom, he would be all right.

"We got this," he repeated quietly.

"Exactly," she said with a smile. "Now let's get you down to the car."

She helped him sit up on the snowboard, then started pulling him slowly down the hill.

"How did you know I was even up here?" Rowan asked, now that his senses were about him.

"You're not as quiet as you think," she said with a laugh. "I heard the front door close as you left."

"Are you mad?" he whispered.

"I'm not mad," she said. "But I know how smart you are—and that you know how important it is to tell me where you're going."

Rowan nodded. "Yeah, that was pretty dumb."

His mother turned back to him. "Not dumb, no. You'll just learn from this for next time, okay?"

Rowan nodded, wincing at the pain still radiating from his wrist.

"I'm glad you were here, Mom," he said quietly.

"Me too, honey."

PRIORITIZING CONNECTION OVER STRESS

*** Kenta

Kenta sat in his mom's lap in the ER waiting room, still shivering with cold. She pulled the blanket a little tighter around him, and he leaned into her.

"How long are they going to keep us waiting?" his dad said. Kenta could feel the nervous energy radiating off of him, and it made him feel even more guilty for putting his parents through this.

Suddenly, the doors opened and a woman rushed in, carrying a boy who looked to be about Kenta's age. He was pale, and his arm was covered in blood. A nurse ran over to look at him, then immediately took him back.

"Why does he get to go first?" Kenta's dad shouted, jumping up from his chair. "Our son needs help too!"

"Don't make a scene," his mom mumbled, pulling her husband back down to his seat.

"Kenta Tanaka?" a nurse soon called out.

"That's us!" Kenta's parents jumped up, nearly knocking Kenta over as his weak legs struggled to hold him upright.

"What's going on?" the nurse asked as she led them to an open room.

"Our son thought it'd be a good idea to swim in the lake for some reason," Kenta's mom said as she pushed Kenta toward the nurse. "He's still ice cold to the touch. We think he might have hypothermia!"

Kenta's mother was in full-blown panic now, and she wasn't trying to hide it. And the more anxiety she expelled, the more her son absorbed.

"I'm...v-very... cold," Kenta whispered, his shaking somehow becoming even more pronounced.

"We'll get you all warmed up soon," the nurse said, guiding Kenta into the bed.

*** Rowan

Down the hall, Rowan had been shown to a room with another patient, a light fabric curtain dividing the space. Rowan and his mother could hear the beeping of machines attached to the man next to them.

Rowan's nurse, who'd introduced herself as Judy, had been asking questions about the accident. When she moved Rowan's arm slightly, he suddenly got very dizzy and nearly fainted.

"Did he hit his head? Melissa, we may have a brain bleed here!" Judy shouted out the door.

"I'm not sure. I didn't see it happen," his mother responded calmly.

Another nurse came over and started speaking to Judy just outside Rowan's door. "What are his symptoms? Has he had a seizure? Is he vomiting? Can he feel his extremities?" she asked.

Each word out of the nurse's mouth built more fear in Rowan. "Mom, I don't want to die," Rowan cried.

Rowan's mother smoothed his hair down. "You're not going to die, honey. Look at how far you've come already! You made it down the hill, through the car ride, and now we're almost there. You're okay."

With each stroke of his mother's hand, Rowan felt his body relax a tiny bit more.

*** Kenta

Back in Kenta's room, after the nurse left, Kenta's parents talked among themselves. But Kenta could still hear. He could always hear.

"I just don't know what he was thinking," his father huffed.

"He was just so blue…" his mother said.

As her husband continued on, Kenta's mother found her mind drifting to a memory from her own childhood. She'd been on a canoe with her brother. She'd been having so much fun, and then suddenly, the canoe flipped. The water was deeper and faster than she thought, and she couldn't get to the surface…

Kenta's mother shook her head, trying to get rid of the image that still plagued her nightmares decades later. That primal fear within her arose and her panic about Kenta grew tenfold.

She walked away from her husband and over to Kenta's bed. "You can't do stupid stuff like this, Kenta! This could have been very bad. You could have died!" She could barely catch her breath as the anxiety built more and more.

Her husband came over and put his arm around her. "She's right. You have to be smarter than that, son."

Despite still feeling near-frozen, Kenta's cheeks burned with shame.

*** Rowan

Rowan was taking deep breaths with his mother when a machine from the patient next to them started beeping loudly. The dividing curtain wasn't pulled over all the way, and Rowan and his mother could see a man lying in the bed with his eyes closed. His arms were thrashing, and a nurse hurried in to calm him down. Rowan and his mother could see that the man had matching bandages wrapped around his wrists.

Judy came over and pulled the curtain closed, ending their line of sight.

"What happened to him?" Rowan asked, his curiosity getting the best of him.

The nurse leaned close and whispered, "He was in an accident. We're doing everything we can."

Judy stepped out of the room, and Rowan and his mother found themselves alone with this unknown man.

"It's sad he's all alone," Rowan said.

"It is. What if we put our energy into helping him heal? We can close our eyes and think really good thoughts and send them his way," Rowan's mom suggested.

Rowan closed his eyes, but soon winced in pain. "Mom, my arm hurts too much. I can't think about anything else."

His mother leaned close. "Remember how we've talked about the superpower of focusing your mind? If we can focus our attention on helping this man, even for a minute, it's going to magically help with your pain, too."

Rowan nodded and closed his eyes tight.

*** Kenta

Kenta's fingers were finally starting to regain their strength. He could almost make a fist under the layers of covers piled on top of him.

The doctor came into the room, holding Kenta's chart. "Looks like he's starting to warm up, which is great. But I did want to talk about the potential of pneumonia."

"I didn't even think about that. He could be sick for months!" Kenta's mother exclaimed.

"Well, let's not get ahead of ourselves. We're still monitoring..."

Kenta's mother moved closer to the bedside. "How do your lungs feel, Kenta? Can you take a deep breath?"

Kenta tried to inhale deeply, but it suddenly felt like the blankets weighed fifty pounds each. What had he been thinking? Of course the lake was too cold to swim in. He should have known that. And he could have died! Even now, he could still be sick for months. He couldn't swim if he was sick! Now he'd let his parents down, his teammates down, his coach down... all so he could try to get in a stupid practice swim.

With each thought, Kenta's heart raced harder. Soon he could only manage short, shallow breaths.

"Look, he can barely breathe!" his mother said, pointing to her nearly hyperventilating son.

"Calm down, Kenta! You're only making things worse by panicking," his dad ordered.

Kenta watched as the doctor tried to explain the symptoms to his parents, but he was no longer listening.

He thought he deserved this discomfort, this pain. It was his own damn fault.

*** Rowan

A few minutes went by, and Judy re-entered Rowan's room. "Oh, I'm sorry. I didn't mean to interrupt," she said, seeing Rowan and his mother with their eyes closed and heads bent down.

"It's okay, we were just sending good thoughts to my room neighbor," Rowan said.

"Well, that's very kind of both of you. I'm sure he appreciates it." The nurse looked over to Rowan's mother and smiled. "But we're all prepped, so it's time to take you in for surgery. Your mom will be right here waiting for you when you're done."

Rowan's eyes grew big. His mom leaned down to kiss his forehead.

"Mom, I'm scared," Rowan whispered.

"You know what honey? It's okay to be scared. You just went through a scary moment. But look how brave you're being! You made it down the mountain. You've sat through all of Judy's questions. And you've even helped another patient feel better! And now *you* get to go get better. And remember what we talked about on the mountain? What did we say?"

"We got this."

"That's right. We got this." Rowan's mom kissed his forehead again and gave a nod to the nurse, who started wheeling Rowan out.

Once Rowan was out of the room, his mom released a heavy sigh. The pent-up tears started rolling down her cheeks. As she rubbed her eyes, she heard the patient next door cough.

She sat for a moment, looking at the drawn, scratchy-looking curtain. Right now, she couldn't do anything more for Rowan. But she could do something for this hurting stranger.

Slipping behind the curtain, Rowan's mother walked over to the man. His eyes opened a slit.

"Can I sit with you?" she asked, her voice a soothing whisper.

The man nodded slowly. His eyes closed again.

She pulled a chair up to the bed and took a seat. Now she got a better view of the bandages around his wrists. She also saw his name on his hospital bracelet: Pierre.

She wondered what Pierre must have been through to attempt to end it all.

She steadied her breath and closed her eyes.

While she tried to relay positive thoughts, she found herself getting transported back to her own dark days. Her eighteenth birthday, when her parents kicked her out of the house. The nights she spent sleeping in the train station. The night Rowan's father said he wasn't interested in being a dad.

Then, as quickly as the hard memories came, the remarkable moments started flooding in. Her first day at the women's shelter. The warmth and acceptance she felt for the first time in her life. The day of Rowan's birth. The realization that every one of us has something beautiful and special to offer the world.

Rowan's mother felt a familiar serenity pour over her, and a muted smile instinctively crossed her lips. In her bones, she knew what she wanted to do.

"I don't know your story," she whispered, "but I know how tough the world can be. And I want you to know that you matter to me."

The man's hand slowly moved toward her. She took his hand in hers and felt him grip it gently. They sat together like this for an hour, in silence, letting the significance of this moment sink in.

While many of us didn't grow up with a parent or role model like Rowan's mom, it's not too late to absorb her teachings. That's exactly what this book aims to do: teach you to let go of the myth of correction and practice a way of living by connection.

Before we can move into this connection-first mindset, we need to fully understand how correction has shaped the way we interact in our daily lives. We need to create an awareness of the individual False Belonging Habits each of us operate out of every day. And who better to teach us than Kenta and Rowan themselves?

Let's catch up with them again, now several decades later.

CHAPTER 2

KENTA: HOOKED ON PERFORMANCE

"And here we have the design for the waiting room area." Kenta said, pointing to the slide with his sketches. As he spoke, he watched the faces of the partners and the client. They nodded and smiled, seemingly impressed.

Good. That's what he wanted to see.

But then Kenta's father, a partner at the firm, raised his eyebrows. Why did he do that? Did he not like the rounded shape Kenta recommended for the front desk? Kenta decided to preemptively defend himself. "The curved edge of the desk gives a softer feel for the customers entering the room," he explained.

For the rest of the presentation, he upped his charm. He was as well-spoken as he could possibly be. By the time he finished the presentation, he felt like he had nailed it, as usual.

Then it was Becca's turn to present her design. "I wanted to bring a modern feel to the office, one that has customers feeling like they have an *experience* upon entering the building."

Kenta kept a reserved smile on his face, watching the audience out of the side of his eye. Was the client smiling more at Becca's presentation than she had at his? Why hadn't he gone more modern? He had considered it. To be honest, he'd spent many evenings working late, thinking through all kinds of designs: modern, traditional, something in between.

This wasn't unusual for Kenta. He never did anything half-assed, and this meticulous work ethic usually paid off for him. It's how he'd gotten to his senior-level position so quickly. He'd never lost a proposal. That couldn't change now, could it?

A few hours later, Kenta was reading through an email in his office when his father knocked on the door.

"You busy?"

"No, come in," Kenta said. He sat up straighter, as he always did around his father.

"The client decided which design they're going with." His father sighed. "It's Becca's."

It felt like someone had squeezed all the air from Kenta's lungs. "Oh."

"I really wanted to advocate for yours, Kenta, but... she just knocked it out of the park."

"I see," Kenta said, trying to hide his disappointment.

"I hate to say it, but it seems like you're slipping, son."

"I mean, this is the first proposal I've lost..." Kenta began.

"It's a slippery slope," his father cut in. "I'm not going to be here forever. You can't have another slipup like this if you want to get partner. Got it?"

Kenta could feel the familiar burn of shame in his cheeks. He would normally defend his idea, his abilities, his intelligence. But it was different with his father—especially when they were at work.

So, Kenta remained silent.

His father exhaled loudly. "You're still going to the gallery for that architecture exhibit tonight, right? It'll look good for you to be there with your coworkers."

"Yeah, I was planning on it."

"Good. That's good." His father nodded. "Well, I've got to get back to work. Look over Becca's design again if you get a chance. You might learn something."

Kenta sat staring at his desk as the door closed, still in shock. The disappointment from his father hung thickly in the air like a pungent cologne. Kenta felt sick to his stomach. Everyone had laughed at Becca's jokes; he could have tried to incorporate some humor, too. He definitely should have tried to make his design more modern.

He should have tried *harder.*

Kenta's False Belonging Habit: I believe if I perform well, and I get outside recognition, I will belong.

Can you relate? Do you feel like your goals take priority in your life?

PERFORMANCE MEETS OPPORTUNITY FOR CHANGE

Kenta smiled at his coworker's comment, taking another swig from his Manhattan. The last place he wanted to be was here, pretending everything was okay.

Pretending he wasn't an absolute wreck on the inside.

"Hey Becca, I just gotta say your idea for that glass wall next to the stairwell? Genius," a colleague said. Kenta smiled through gritted teeth before taking another drink.

"Thanks! I was just looking for something outside the norm, you know? Something that hadn't been done a hundred times before," Becca said.

Was that a dig at Kenta's design? He thought his ideas had been just as innovative, maybe even more so. But of course he didn't say that; he had a reputation to uphold. "It really was a great design, Becca. Congrats. Does anyone else need another drink?" Kenta asked the group.

They shook their heads, a few glancing down at their still nearly full glasses.

"I'll be right back then," Kenta said with a smile. He turned and walked briskly toward the door.

As soon as he was in the hallway, Kenta threw his head back and sighed. He loosened his tie, wishing he could chuck it across the floor. But then, automatically, he straightened it back up. A successful man had to keep it together. He made his way to a decorative mirror in the hall and gave himself a quick once-over, smoothing a stray piece of his short black hair back into his sleek, professional hairstyle.

Kenta continued on his way to the bar, where a long line snaked next to grand paintings on the wall. As he waited, he tipped his glass all the way back, not wanting any drop of his drink to go to waste. Liquid confidence.

"Excuse me," Kenta heard a voice behind him say, "You seem to have something on your jacket."

Kenta twisted his head around to look down. A giant splotch of white powder, most likely from the chalk he used at the office, was smeared across the bottom half of the back of his jacket. How long had he been walking around like that? Hours?

"Oh wow. Yeah, thanks," Kenta mumbled, quickly patting away the powder. "That's so embarrassing."

"Hey, it's happened to the best of us. I once unknowingly walked out of the kitchen with my sleeve dripping in soy sauce."

"Well, thanks for letting me know," Kenta said, finally looking up at the man.

"Rowan," the man said, extending his hand.

"Kenta," he answered, shaking Rowan's hand. Unlike everyone else here, Rowan wore jeans and a plaid button-down shirt, standing out among all the suits and ties. "Are you here for the architecture exhibit?" Kenta asked, eyeing the slow-moving line in front of him.

"Yes, I am! I was walking by and saw the sign, so I thought I'd check it out."

Rowan was exuding such warmth, genuine kindness, and happiness that Kenta couldn't help but get drawn in.

"Nice! I'm here with some colleagues from our firm. Are you also an architect?"

"Oh, no," Rowan chuckled. "I own a restaurant."

Kenta's eyes lit up. "Oh, that must be a blast! Which one?"

"The Hearth."

Kenta could barely contain himself. "I've heard of that! Your duck confit is supposed to be out of this world."

"Well, I think it's pretty good," Rowan said with a smile. "Most people can't pronounce it though. I'm impressed!"

Kenta felt that oh-so-familiar tingle throughout his body at receiving even the smallest validation. "I did study cooking for a bit, so I should know how to say it."

"Oh? Where did you study?"

Kenta's smile now became forced. "Informally, I mean. It's a hobby of mine."

Kenta watched Rowan's reaction. Did he think Kenta was just some wannabe chef? Any part of him that was impressed with Kenta's pronunciation must have disappeared. Kenta despised appearing like an amateur—in anything.

But Rowan just smiled, without the least bit of judgment in his eyes. "Well, just because it's a hobby doesn't mean you didn't study it. Have you been cooking for a long time?"

"Yeah, I used to cook with my grandma as a kid. She was first-generation Japanese, so we'd make udon and dumplings and all that good stuff from scratch. We'd spend hours in the kitchen every weekend," Kenta replied, a wide, reminiscent smile on his face.

Kenta didn't get to talk about cooking much. At work, he was always focused on the task at hand. Or schmoozing. And then in his social life... well, that was nonexistent with all the extra hours he'd been putting in at work.

"Sounds like you would have made quite the chef if you hadn't been an architect," Rowan added.

"Well, in my family, being a chef wasn't really an option," Kenta joked with an uncomfortable laugh. He looked forward again, thankful to almost be at the front of the line.

"Oh? Why's that?"

Kenta turned back to Rowan. "Oh, you know... My dad's an architect, wanted me to follow in his footsteps. I didn't have much of a say in it," Kenta said with another uncomfortable laugh. Then he quickly added, "Not that I minded. I'm poised to reach partner before long."

"So you like it?"

"What?" Kenta asked, caught off guard.

"You like being an architect?" Rowan asked.

"Well..." Kenta stuttered. "As much as anyone likes their 9 to 5." He tried to make light of the comment, but it wasn't landing.

"I love my 9 to 5," Rowan said, without any hesitation.

For a moment, Kenta allowed himself to picture what an average workday must look like for Rowan: the fast pace of the kitchen, the experimenting with ingredients, the camaraderie with the other chefs.

Honestly, it sounded like heaven.

But Kenta quickly shook away that image. "Yes. I mean, I do too."

Rowan nodded, watching Kenta closely. "Can I ask a favor?" Rowan inquired. "Would you be willing to come to my restaurant and show me how to make dumplings?"

Kenta couldn't help but grin at the idea. But then he remembered how much work he had to get done. "I mean, I don't know..."

"Well, how about I give you my card, just in case," Rowan said. To be polite, Kenta offered Rowan his business card as well.

"I hope to hear from you soon, Kenta," Rowan said just as the bartender finished with the customer in front of them. It seemed like he genuinely meant it.

"Yeah. Nice to meet you." After Kenta was done ordering his drink, he turned around and gave Rowan one last nod, then made his way back to his colleagues.

On the walk, Kenta couldn't help but think back to that tempting image of spending a day cooking in a kitchen. But as he neared his coworkers, the vision was replaced by dread. Kenta really didn't want to be around them anymore, but he couldn't let that show. He could never let any weakness show. So, he plastered on his smile, took a deep breath, and headed back into the room.

A week after the exhibit, Kenta got a call from a local number he didn't know. "Hello?"

"Kenta! It's Rowan. I just wanted to check if you'd still be open to coming down to The Hearth?"

Kenta held back a sigh. He had hoped it was a potential new client, or something else that would help him get ahead. "I'm so slammed at the office, I don't know if I have the time."

"I get that," Rowan said. "But I've always found that cooking gives my mind a nice break, if you think that could be helpful?"

Kenta nearly laughed aloud. He'd been working even harder after losing that proposal to Becca; his mind had never needed more of a break than it did now.

"I could show you how we prepare some of our dishes, too. Like that duck confit you mentioned," Rowan added.

Now, Kenta perked up. If he could level up his cooking game, then this wouldn't be some frivolous visit. It'd have a purpose. He'd be expanding his skill set. And there was just something about Rowan that made Kenta want to get to know him more.

"Okay, you've got a deal," Kenta agreed.

"Excellent!" Rowan cheered. "Could you come by next Tuesday before we open for dinner? Say around three?"

Kenta normally didn't like to leave work early, but he could always start work early to even it out. "Sure thing," he said. "I can make that work." As he spoke, he made a calendar event to get to work by 6:30 a.m. on Tuesday.

"Awesome!" Rowan sounded genuinely excited. "Just text me a list of the ingredients you'll need. Looking forward to it!"

Kenta couldn't help but smile. "Me too, Rowan. See you then."

DELVING INTO AUTHENTICITY

Kenta's nerves were high as he knocked on the front door of the restaurant. He was majorly second-guessing if coming here was a good idea.

Rowan opened the door enthusiastically. "Kenta! Great to see you!"

Kenta was much more at ease once they crossed the threshold. Loud Spanish music emanated from the back of the restaurant, and the air smelled of fresh-baked bread. The two headed back to the kitchen where a young woman was busy chopping vegetables.

"Kenta, this is Mia," Rowan said.

Kenta raised his hand in a polite greeting that Mia acknowledged with a nod. "Hola!" she said, raising her voice above the music.

"We're just prepping for tonight's dinner," Rowan explained. "But please, make yourself at home. Feel free to carve out a workstation anywhere you can. Here's the groceries you asked for," he said, handing Kenta a box with green onions sticking out of the top.

As Kenta found an area of open stainless steel counter and unloaded his groceries, he found himself experiencing an almost childlike wonder at the fancy, commercial-grade equipment.

Meanwhile, Rowan started singing along to the song playing. As he chopped veggies alongside Mia, his feet danced a mini salsa.

"Here we go!" Mia yelled as the beat picked up, doing her own dance.

"C'mon, Kenta! Join in!" Rowan invited.

Kenta hesitated. He didn't consider himself much of a dancer. And the idea of looking like a fool in front of these two new people sounded awful. He made a mental note to read up on tips for dancing.

26

"So," Mia asked, ignoring Kenta's choice to not dance, "you're an architect, right? What kind of buildings do you design?"

"None right now," Kenta blurted sarcastically. Then he paused. He couldn't believe he'd just said that! "I mean..." He sighed. "A client just chose my coworker's design over mine, so I'm in between projects."

"Were you happy with what you designed?" Rowan asked.

"Well, yeah. Before I presented it, at least."

"Then you and the client just have different tastes. There's nothing wrong with that."

Kenta looked up from washing his vegetables and gave Rowan a funny look. "I hadn't thought of it that way."

Out of the corner of his eye, Kenta saw Mia look at the two of them and smirk.

"Something to consider in the future then, huh?" Rowan suggested.

"I guess so," Kenta said. He started to feel more at ease among these strangers. As the three continued to work alongside one another, they got to talking and sharing stories, mostly about their love of food and cooking. Kenta showed Rowan how to make his grandma's famous pork dumplings, and to his surprise, Rowan deferred completely to Kenta's knowledge, despite clearly being a gifted and experienced chef.

"Oh, you mix these together first? I wouldn't have thought to do that," Rowan commented.

"Actually, my mom came up with that. It's pretty brilliant, right?" Kenta asked. "Now, for this bit, we need to chop these very fine."

As time went on, Kenta found that he didn't want the afternoon to end. For some reason, there was less pressure here than with most social gatherings. Kenta didn't feel that ever-present need to tell the perfect joke or be the most outgoing person in the room. He didn't need to be "the best" in this kitchen. He could just be another one of the chefs, and that was... refreshing.

Finally, it was time to taste the dumplings. Kenta could feel that familiar pressure weighing down on him as he, Mia, and Rowan each took their first bite. To Kenta's relief, the dumplings were spot-on. They had the absolute perfect consistency, had the right amount of spice, and were chock-full of flavor. They may have been the best dumplings he had ever made.

"Wow!" Kenta said after swallowing the first bite. He tended to talk himself up without even thinking about it.

"Delicious!" Rowan said.

"Mmm, they're great," Mia added, shoving the rest of her dumpling into her mouth.

"I'm so glad you came in to show us how to make these," Rowan added.

Kenta was glowing. He wondered what else they were going to say.

But to his surprise, Rowan changed the subject. "Now let's get working on these dishes so we're not here until midnight!"

As they moved toward the sink, Kenta tried to keep the topic of his dumplings alive. "You know, I think your pan really made all the difference. They've never been that crispy at home."

"That could be," Rowan said.

Now Kenta was starting to second-guess himself. Did the dumplings not taste as good as he thought?

"Maybe I'll sauté the garlic longer next time. What do you think?"

Rowan shook his head. "I think they were good as is."

But Kenta didn't want them to just be *good*; he wanted them to be *great*. "Or maybe I should add more filling next time?"

Rowan finally looked up from stacking the dishes. "What did *you* think of the dumplings, Kenta?"

"Um, well, I thought they were good."

"Exactly. You have a good instinct for cooking. Trust your gut."

Mia and Rowan continued chatting as they cleaned up, but Kenta was unusually quiet. Why didn't he ever just trust his gut? Why was he so hell-bent on having Rowan and Mia tell him how good his food was when he already knew the answer?

Once they finished, Kenta said, "I just wanted to thank you again for inviting me over here, Rowan. I've had such an amazing afternoon."

"Well, you've proved yourself to be quite the chef. You're welcome to stop by and cook with us anytime," Rowan responded, smiling.

Kenta was relieved. Rowan really *had* been sincere when he said he liked Kenta's food. He wouldn't have invited Kenta back if he wasn't.

Kenta felt torn between two emotions: joy at the prospect of coming back and cooking at The Hearth, and aggravation at himself for not being able to believe in his own abilities. In that moment, he made a promise to himself: the next time he came to cook, he wasn't going to fish for a compliment. And that idea filled him with both peace and anxiety.

TRADING PERFORMANCE FOR PASSION

The day after his successful trip to The Hearth, Kenta surprised himself by calling Rowan to ask if he could cook at the kitchen again next weekend. Rowan agreed, and over the next few months Kenta became a mainstay at The Hearth whenever he wasn't working. He came by every weekend and even took a sick day from the firm to help cater a Thursday night wedding.

The more Kenta cooked, the more fulfilled he felt. For the first time in his adult life, he didn't feel like he was just going through the motions. He felt invigorated and happy, even though he was keeping this part of his life a secret from his family and colleagues.

"I've been thinking about what it would look like if I started cooking full time, like we talked about," Kenta said to Rowan one day as they were preparing appetizers. "But then I get caught thinking about having to tell my parents."

"How do you think that would go?" Rowan asked.

"Well, in every scenario, I see them disowning me," Kenta said.

Rowan took a moment before responding. "Well, have you imagined what will happen if you continue to play out the scenario you're living in right now? The one in which you keep working at the firm and never say a word to them about how you really feel?"

Kenta stopped chopping for a moment. "No, I guess I haven't pictured that... wow. You know, I can't even envision that anymore—me still working at the firm ten years from now. Even five years from now. I think you've corrupted me," Kenta joked.

"Hey now! I've only offered my kitchen. Everything else was you," Rowan responded with a laugh.

"Can I get some help?" Mia yelled, barging through the door with a dripping box.

As Kenta grabbed a towel, he couldn't help but replay Rowan's comment in his mind. And as he did, he realized something: he already had this love of cooking inside of him, and he'd been ignoring it his whole life.

⊶+⊷

Deep down, Kenta knew that he couldn't keep this up forever. Eventually, someone would find out about his side job, and then everyone would know what he was up to, including his parents. But for now, he kept kicking that can further and further down the road.

Then, one Saturday night, his worst fear became a reality.

Kenta was cooking in the back when he heard an unmistakable laugh coming from the packed dining room. He poked his head out the kitchen door and immediately spotted one of the waitresses chatting with his parents, who had obviously come for dinner.

Kenta closed the door as gently as possible, then leaned against a nearby counter. He suddenly felt like he was on fire, with sweat starting to build on his lower back. His stomach started doing cartwheels, and it took everything for him to remain upright.

His two worlds were colliding, and Kenta had to decide: should he hide? Or face his reality?

Spotting Kenta's reaction from across the room, Rowan rushed over to his friend. "You okay?"

For a split second, Kenta considered not telling Rowan. But as he looked at Rowan's concerned eyes, he relaxed ever so slightly. If anyone could help him through a moment like this, it was Rowan.

"My parents are out there," Kenta whispered.

"Oh... didn't expect that," Rowan said. "How are you feeling?"

31

"Not great."

"Well, how can I help?"

Kenta smirked unconsciously. "Thanks, but I think I need to decide this one on my own."

The next hour was excruciating for Kenta. One moment, he'd decide to just keep on cooking and not say anything to them. The next moment, he was admonishing himself for being a chicken and determined to go tell them everything. With every new decision came a new wave of anxiety. There was no perfect answer, and the stress was eating Kenta up inside.

As Mia walked out to the dining room with a tray full of food, Kenta peered out to check on his parents. To his dismay, their table was now empty.

Kenta swore under his breath. As painful as them being here had been, at least *he* was the one making a decision. Now he felt devoid of power and mad at himself.

Something in Kenta told him to see if he could catch them. He told Rowan he was taking a break and took off out the back door. He hightailed it to the sidewalk—and came face to face with his parents.

"Kenta?" his mother asked, giving him an odd look.

"Hi," Kenta responded, his anxiety spiking.

"Why are you dressed like that?" his dad asked.

Kenta tried to steady his breath. It didn't work well. "Well... I've been cooking here on the weekends and some nights for a few months now. I, um, haven't told you because I didn't know how you'd respond."

Kenta kept his eyes down, focused on his kneading hands.

"Why?" his dad asked, bewildered.

"Because," Kenta said, finally looking his father in the eye, "I love to cook. I always have. Mom, when we'd cook with grandma,

I was in absolute heaven. It was my favorite part of my childhood, and that love for food hasn't gone away."

Kenta took a deep breath. "And that's what makes this so hard. I know how much you've sacrificed for me. Dad—all the help studying for my architecture tests. Mom—the never-ending after-school activities to get into a good school. I so appreciate everything you've both done for me, but I feel like it's time for me to pursue this."

"So, you'll... moonlight as a cook?" his mom asked.

"Well, um, kind of..." Kenta trailed off. He was starting to lose his nerve. He inhaled slowly to calm his mind; it was now or never. "No. I want to cook full time."

"You're going to throw away everything you've worked for? Everything we've worked for?" his dad exclaimed, shaking his head.

A tense silence fell over the group. Kenta swallowed, hoping his parents would say something, anything. But the couple simply shared a look, seemingly communicating without saying a word.

"It's getting late. Your mother and I need to head home. We'll... talk about this later," his father said.

Kenta nodded. "I understand." They exchanged terse goodbyes, and then Kenta watched them walk away. Kenta's father reached over and held his wife's hand. She leaned into her husband, and they disappeared around a corner.

As he watched this scene, Kenta felt an odd wave of calm pass over him. He had spoken up to his parents, and the world hadn't stopped. The ground didn't break open and suck Kenta down into it. His parents didn't faint at the shock of what he said.

His parents left. And that was it.

For the first time, Kenta saw his parents not as Mom and Dad, but as two fully functioning adults—just like him. His mother was a brilliant woman who made caring for and protecting her family her priority. His dad was a man who worked so hard to achieve what he had, and who wanted to pass down that good fortune to his son.

Yet, Kenta noticed that he didn't want to run after them to tell them that he changed his mind. For once, he didn't feel the need to be the perfect son.

Surprised, Kenta headed back inside. Rowan and Mia were waiting for him.

"Did you see them?" Mia asked, sounding concerned.

Kenta nodded. "I... told them everything."

"How are you feeling?" Rowan asked.

Kenta was about to respond, but he paused. He hadn't actually asked himself that yet. His heart was racing, but it wasn't the usual crushing anxiety. It was a different kind of energy—an *excited* energy.

"Is it weird I feel good?"

A MOMENT IN THE MIRROR: HOOKED ON PERFORMANCE

Can you recognize Kenta's False Belonging Habit—**I believe if I perform well, and I get outside recognition, I will belong**—within yourself?

Like Kenta, many of us have been taught that it's important to succeed within the expectations the world places on us. On one hand, being driven and pushing ourselves can be great qualities to have; these characteristics can help us attain our goals and dreams! But when we tie our self-worth to that success, we fall out of balance. We develop a pattern of performing because we think *this* is the way to experience approval and be seen. We tie being a superstar to belonging.

To better understand if this False Belonging Habit applies to you, try to answer the following questions honestly and without self-criticism.

1. Are you an overachiever? Do you keep pushing and pushing, relegating relationships to get to the goal?
2. Do you seek to be recognized by others?
3. Do you compare yourself to others and their accomplishments?
4. Do you get jealous of others' achievements?
5. Do you fall into despair if you don't achieve your aim, but then hide your anguish?
6. Are you seldom satisfied with your success? Do you have a tendency to say, "I could do more"?

We have begun the journey of learning about the six False Belonging Habits. As mentioned earlier, the invitation is to explore for yourself and see which speaks to you. Now we will meet Amani, who has a distinctly different ingrained Habit.

CHAPTER 3

AMANI: NEGLECTING ONESELF

Amani looked through her paperwork as she hurried through the halls of the outpatient addiction clinic where she was interning.

"Amani!" her supervisor called from her office as Amani rushed by, bringing her to a halt. "Guess what?" her supervisor asked with a huge smile.

"What?" Amani asked, her own grin growing.

"It turns out that Blake had some personal stuff come up, so he can't present at the conference. So, I brought your name up, and… everyone agreed you'd be a great replacement!"

"Gabby! Are you serious?" Amani nearly shrieked, throwing her hands over her mouth.

"Yes! You've been working your butt off. You earned it."

Amani was shaking from excitement. "I mean, we've talked about how much I've wanted to present someday, but I didn't think it'd happen this soon! This is just amazing."

Her boss smiled. "I'll email you the details. You're gonna kill it."

"Thanks again! I'll do my best!" Amani beelined to her office to read up on the details. She couldn't believe it. Yes, she'd helped Blake with basically the entire presentation, but now *she* would get to present what she'd spent so long helping put together.

Amani couldn't keep the grin off her face as she plopped down in front of her computer. As she waited for the incoming email, she started brainstorming some of her talking points. Soon, she saw the new message and excitedly opened it. And that's when her heart dropped.

The conference was Thursday afternoon. The same time as the semifinals for her son's high school soccer team.

"Shit," she grumbled. She got up and hurried to close her office door.

Her hand still on the doorknob, she closed her eyes tight, trying to keep the tears from flooding out. *What kind of mother would I be if I missed Luke's game?* she thought.

But that didn't keep the disappointment from kicking her in the gut.

"I would have crushed that presentation," she muttered. She slid down to the floor, sitting in a ball as the tears finally broke through their barrier. She didn't let herself stay there for long, though. *You don't have time for this,* she told herself. *You have to meet up with the clients.*

Rising slowly from the floor, Amani looked at a small glittery purple mirror she had hung on the wall. The face of a defeated woman looked back at her. She shook her head and wiped away the tears; she didn't have time to worry about her little troubles. She shot off an email to her boss explaining how she wouldn't be able to present due to a previous engagement, then marched out the door. Her clients had *real* issues, and as long as she was helping them, she was at least doing something right.

Amani's False Belonging Habit: I believe if I put others' needs and expectations above my own, I will belong.

Can you relate? How often do you feel depleted from prioritizing the needs of others over your own?

THE PAIN OF SELF-NEGLECT

"You all head in! I'll be there in a minute," Amani told the van full of clients as she pulled into the restaurant parking lot.

Amani had been trying her hardest to focus on the clients in the car. These folks were so inspiring to her. Despite going through their issues with addiction, they were trying so hard to turn their lives around, and Amani was there to do whatever she could to help them succeed. And right now, that meant driving them to a cooking class downtown.

Yet her mind kept wandering to the email she'd sent to her boss, turning down the opportunity to present at the conference. Her boss had replied, but Amani couldn't bring herself to read it.

As she watched the restaurant door close behind the group, she let her head fall forward to rest on the steering wheel. This was exactly the kind of thing she'd worried about when deciding whether to go back to school: that her kids' needs and her work requirements would clash. She'd been able to balance everything pretty well last semester, if you didn't count the fact that she averaged five hours of sleep a night. But this semester, her final semester, her internship at the clinic was complicating matters. The late hours made it impossible to cook dinner for her family most nights, or to help the kids with their homework. And now she was literally being forced to choose between the two biggest priorities in her life.

She glanced at the clock and realized she'd been in the car alone for a few minutes already. *Time to focus on the group. Just let it go for now.* With that, she shook herself off, turned on her smile, and headed inside.

By the time Amani walked in, the group was already gathered around the prep table, listening intently to the volunteer who led the class. "For this gluten-free bread, we need to make sure the yeast... oh! Who do we have here?"

Amani felt her face grow hot. "Oh, I'm just the driver! Please carry on," she said, adjusting her glasses.

"Just the driver!" a client said in feigned disbelief. "You're more than that, Amani!"

"Who stayed late last week to wait with me when my ride was late?" one asked.

"And who helped me work up the nerve to finally call my dad?" another said.

The rest of the group joined in, and Amani waved them down with her hands. "Okay, okay! Thanks everybody," she said with a laugh. "I'm Amani."

"Nice to meet you, Amani! I'm Rowan."

"Please continue," Amani said quickly, with a dismissive wave of her hand.

Rowan began leading the group through the dough-making process. As they kneaded, Amani could see how comfortable the group felt around him. One normally quiet client started speaking about a bakery he used to visit as a child. That inspired another to talk about the sugar cookies his grandma used to make at Christmastime.

"What about you, Amani?" Rowan asked. "Bake with your parents much?"

Amani thought about it for a moment. "When I was little, yeah. Peanut butter cookies were my mom's specialty." She smiled at the memory of scooping the goopy peanut butter into the batter. "I haven't thought about that in a long time. That was before she got sick," she said, more to herself than anything.

"Oh?" Rowan asked.

Amani didn't want to be rude, so she responded. "Yeah, uh,

breast cancer. Pretty bad, actually. So, no more cookie-making nights after that. Instead, I became the master of making soup!" Amani said, trying to lighten the mood.

"That must have been hard," Rowan said.

"Oh, once I got into a routine it wasn't too bad. After school I'd get Mom her meds, make sure my brothers did their homework, made dinner—not too different from today, I suppose."

"So you were a teenager then, when all this happened?" Rowan asked.

"No, I was eleven."

The mood in the room shifted. "That's a lot on a kid's shoulders," Rowan said gently.

"Yeah, well. If I didn't do it, it wouldn't get done," Amani said.

"Not really fair you didn't have anyone to take care of *you*, though," one of the clients mumbled.

The word "fair" hit Amani squarely in the chest. She'd always just accepted her childhood as normal; sure, it was busy and tough at times, but she did what she had to. But was what she went through really not fair?

"And look at you now! Still taking care of these wonderful clients. I'd bet you do the lion's share at home too, don't you?" Rowan asked.

"Guilty," Amani joked, still trying to lighten the mood.

"Well, in that case, I hope everyone in your life expresses their gratitude for all you do." By now, everyone had stopped kneading and was simply witnessing this interaction.

Amani's face suddenly grew hot at all the smiling faces looking at her. "Oh yeah, my husband and kids appreciate it. I know they do. Anyway, this isn't about me. Jordan, how's your dough going over here?" Amani wandered over to one of the clients, clearly wanting to shift the focus away from herself.

"Well, I'm not sure if it's supposed to be this runny," Jordan said with a laugh.

Amani released a silent sigh of relief. She couldn't believe she had gone into that stuff about her mom and hogged all the attention. They weren't here to learn about her childhood! She'd make sure to be quiet for the rest of the cooking class so the clients could be the focus.

THE COST OF ABANDONING ONESELF

After the class was over, Amani drove the clients back to the clinic and then went to her office. There was almost nobody else here this late, so she could take a moment to just sit in the peace and quiet.

But the tranquility ended up being *too* quiet. Now there was nothing to distract Amani from the thoughts she kept replaying in her mind. Was her childhood unfair? Did she not receive enough care? Did her family appreciate her now? How long had she been living under the pretense that everything was okay? *Was* everything okay? Wave after wave of emotion crashed over her: guilt, disbelief, anger, sorrow.

The sound of her office phone ringing snapped her out of it. Who could be calling this late?

"Hello?" she answered.

"Hi, this is Rowan over at The Hearth. I have a cell phone here that someone from the class left behind."

Instinctively, Amani reached down to her back jean pocket. It was empty.

"Is the lock screen a photo of three teenagers with a miniature schnauzer?"

"That'd be it!"

"Looks like that's my phone. This is Amani, by the way. Sorry about that. I'll drive over right now to grab it."

"No worries! I was going to be here for a while cleaning up anyway. Take your time," Rowan said.

After she hung up, Amani grabbed her stuff and hurried out as quickly as she could, chastising herself for being so careless. Before long, she was back in the restaurant parking lot. She darted toward the nearest door, which said "Staff Only," and knocked loudly.

"You weren't kidding that you were going to be here soon!" Rowan said, opening the door to let Amani into the kitchen.

"Well, I really didn't want to waste any more of your time. So sorry again," Amani said as Rowan handed her the phone.

"Really, it was no problem." Rowan paused and gave Amani a look that she couldn't quite decipher. "You know, actually, I just pulled this loaf of bazlama out of the oven. Turkish flat bread. Ever had it?"

Amani shook her head, a bit taken aback by the abrupt shift in topic. "I don't think so."

"It's delicious—and best eaten fresh. Would you mind trying a piece and letting me know what you think of it?"

Amani eyed the bread sitting on the counter as the scrumptious scent reached her nose. She felt like she had taken enough of this generous man's time, but it also seemed rude to turn down the offer. "Sure, I'd love to."

Rowan grinned, then went to cut the bread. "Ah, it's still a little too hot. Let's give it a few minutes more. Would you like a glass of water?"

"Yes, please."

As Rowan got a few glasses, the two got to chatting. The more they talked, the more Amani's body calmed down.

"How long have you been a therapist?" Rowan asked.

"Social worker, actually. And social worker *in training*. I'm not certified yet," Amani clarified. "I just went back to school a few years ago. I was a stay-at-home mom for a decade before that."

"How many kids do you have?" Rowan asked.

"Three. I have two daughters in college and a teenage son." Remembering the soccer game debacle, her face suddenly fell.

"Everything okay?" Rowan asked.

"It's just…" Amani sighed. "Luke, my son, has his semifinal soccer game on Thursday."

"That's wonderful!"

"Yeah! It is exciting. There was this work thing I was asked to do, but you know what, the game is definitely more important."

"What work thing?"

"Well, there's this social worker conference in town. I helped my coworker put together a presentation about all the benefits of laughter therapy on mental health..." As Amani spoke, she could feel her energy rising. The more she explained the talk, the more passionate she became. "It'll be great to see what questions come up too, from the audience." Amani caught herself. "I mean it *would* be great to see. I won't be there, so I won't get to hear them."

Yet again, Amani felt like someone had sucker punched her in the gut. She tried to hide her disappointment by pretending to read a recipe framed on the wall.

"Well, I can see your passion about it! And there's no way you can miss the game for the conference?"

"Oh, no," Amani started shaking her head ferociously. "My kids are my number one focus. I always told myself I wouldn't let my work get in the way of being there for them."

"You've had to miss a lot of his other games for work then?" Rowan asked as he cut into the cooled bread.

"Well, no," Amani admitted. "I haven't missed any."

"So this would be the very first game you'd be missing? That doesn't scream 'neglectful parent' to me."

"I guess not. Not like what I went through, right?" Amani sighed. "You know, when Jordan said how the way I grew up wasn't fair... I'd never thought of it that way before. I didn't realize how much I tend to pick up the pieces."

Rowan passed Amani a slice. "Everyone deserves to be supported, Amani. Whether that's a kid helping their mom through sickness, or even the superhero mom who goes to all her son's soc-cer games."

"Yeah," she said, letting her mind trail off.

"In any case, I'd say Luke is pretty lucky to have a mom who comes to ninety-nine percent of his games, even if you did choose to miss one in order to present at this conference."

"Well thank you, it's nice of you to say that," Amani said auto-matically, taking a bite of the bread.

"I didn't mean it as a compliment. It's just the truth. He's a very fortunate kid to have such a loving mother."

Amani suddenly became very uncomfortable. She could feel her body start overheating.

Rowan seemed to notice the sudden change in her demeanor. "Amani? Are you alright?"

"Oh, yes, I'm fine. But I think it's probably time for me to get going. This is very tasty, by the way. Similar to naan, yeah?" Amani asked, walking backward toward the door.

"Yeah, it is," Rowan said.

"Mmm. Well, thanks again!" Amani said, trying to sound cheery. They exchanged goodbyes, and Amani walked briskly to her car.

The full impact of Rowan's statement didn't hit Amani until she was driving home.

"It's just the truth."

Amani tried to wrap her head around it. She *knew* she was a loving mother. Of course she knew that, right? But the most impor-tant part of being a loving mother was being there for your kids, and that thought brought her back to her feeling of dread about missing the conference. She groaned, suddenly feeling overwhelm-ingly tired.

Amani's mind went back to what she had said earlier that night about how much her family appreciates her. She felt a longing to see that acknowledgment played out—to have them directly express their gratitude for all she does for them. But then she dismissed the idea. Her family definitely showed their appreciation for her. Though as she tried to think of an example of them doing so, she came up short.

My brain is just tired, she told herself. *I'm just tired.*

But deep down, she knew that wasn't the truth.

SELF-NEGLECT MEETS ITSELF

By the time Amani got home, her husband and son were already asleep, so she went straight to bed. But even though she was exhausted, she tossed and turned all night. She couldn't stop thinking about missing the conference.

The next morning, Amani's supervisor called her into her office. "I wanted to talk to you about reconsidering speaking at the conference," Gabby said.

Amani's heart dropped. "I really can't. Normally I'd be thrilled! But it's Luke's semifinals and…"

Amani's boss sighed. "Amani, you know how gifted I think you are. Our clients love you. Our staff loves you. You've been taking care of everyone else for so long that you're very good at it. But there's a point where you've got to prioritize what *you* want. Forget about your son for a moment. Do *you* think you'd do well speaking at this conference? Or are we totally misguided?"

"I mean, I think I'd do well."

"Exactly. And, honestly, it's frustrating to hear that. We see how skilled you are, yet you don't seem to want to give yourself the chance to level up."

When the meeting was finally over, Amani felt even worse than she had the night before. Her mind was overwhelmed, and all she wanted was to get away from the barrage of guilty thoughts. She locked herself away in her office to focus on paperwork, even putting a "Do Not Disturb" sign on her doorknob.

When her phone rang, she jumped at the chance for another distraction. "Hello?"

"Amani! It's Rowan. How are you?"

That's not who Amani was expecting. "Well, it's been a day. What can I help you with?"

"I really appreciated you trying that bazlama for me last night. Actually, tonight we're doing a whole night of cooking new recipes. As luck would have it, our taste tester just called out. Any chance you'd be free to come by and try some food?"

"I don't…" Amani caught herself before finishing her thought. She was going to say she couldn't because she had to make dinner for her family. But her boss's words about never doing anything for herself rang in her head. "You know what? Sure. I'd love to. Thanks for the invite."

"That's wonderful!" Rowan's excitement was palpable, and Amani smiled at her decision. This would be fun. And besides, when was the last time she did something just for herself?

NURTURING SELF-WORTH

When Amani arrived at The Hearth, she was surprised to find the parking lot nearly empty. She walked to the front door to find a sign that said "Closing Early for New Recipe Creation." As she entered the dining room, she spotted just two parties left finishing up their meals.

"Amani!" Rowan called to her as he burst out of the kitchen. "So glad you could come. Make yourself at home."

Amani thanked him. "Are there any other taste testers?"

"Just you and us chefs tonight! I need to go check on my dish. Please just relax and enjoy yourself. The first course will be out shortly."

Amani moved toward the kitchen. "Well, at least let me help. I can cut veggies or stir something."

Rowan put up his hands. "No, not at all. You're our guest. Please sit," he said, and then disappeared back into the kitchen.

Amani wandered over to a nearby booth and slowly slid into it. Each minute seemed to drag by. Why was she even here? She could be at home with her family, or at work filing some papers. As she watched the other customers leave, Amani pulled out her phone, about to call her husband, Marcus, and tell him she was coming home.

Just before she hit "Call," Rowan walked out carrying a plate. "Now, this is a new crab cake recipe I made. Let me know what you think."

Crab. Amani's heart sank. Crab was her son's favorite food. He only got it on special occasions, like after a big win.

As she took a bite of the crab cake, Amani's eyes began welling up. "Sorry, it's just hot," she said, wiping away tears.

Rowan looked like he saw right through her. "Is everything okay?"

"Yes, it's very delicious," Amani deflected.

Rowan paused as Amani swallowed the large mouthful. "So, did you change your mind about going to your son's soccer game?"

Amani huffed. This guy could clearly read her pretty well. "Nope." She filled Rowan in on the meeting with her boss. "So, that's where I'm at right now." She shoved the rest of the crab cake into her mouth.

"You know, my mom and I were very close growing up—still are, in fact," Rowan said. "And I remember, one time, I had this huge snowboarding competition, and she wasn't able to make it. And honestly, it still haunts me today."

Amani nearly choked on the crab cake. "Really?"

"No," Rowan said, deadpan. "It sounds like you're an amazing mom, Amani. And I don't think missing a soccer game here and there will take that away from you. But the choice is yours. I mean, you could always go back to being an amazing stay-at-home mom full time…"

Amani scrunched her nose at this suggestion.

"…*or*, you can take the bull by the horns, and go be the best damn social worker there ever was!"

Amani could feel her energy start to match Rowan's. "You know, I do want to be the best damn social worker."

"What was that?" Rowan asked, cupping his hand behind his ear.

Amani laughed. "I want to be the best damn social worker!"

"Woohoo! *Avive la vie!*" Rowan cheered.

Amani was about to ask what that meant when she heard the sound of more hands clapping. She looked over to see a woman and man applauding her.

Amani slid down in her seat, embarrassed again by the attention. "Oh, hi."

"Hi, I'm Mia," said a young woman with a buzzed undercut, giving a small wave.

"I'm Kenta," said the man sitting next to Mia. "Nice to meet you! Rowan, you didn't tell us we have the best damn social worker dining with us."

"I didn't realize it either," Rowan said. "I feel like this calls for the full VIP treatment."

Mia smirked. "Oh yeah?"

Rowan nodded.

"You are in for a treat, Amani!" Kenta said as he dashed to the kitchen.

"I'll grab the rosewater!" Mia said, following right behind him.

Rowan looked back at Amani. "Do you know why I invited you here, Amani?"

She shook her head.

"Because I felt like you could use some time to celebrate *you*. Please, just try to soak this in. You give yourself to everyone else; it's time you took in something for yourself."

From then on, Amani was pampered in a way she never had been. She was served bruschetta, baked brie with figs, and stuffed mushrooms. Between each dish, Mia, Kenta, and Rowan would take turns chatting with her.

"I hope this is all right. I haven't made it this way before," Kenta said, setting down a plate of Moroccan couscous.

"It smells delicious," she said as he sat across from her.

"Are you familiar with Moroccan tradition? Before eating, they create an entirely relaxing ambiance." Kenta pulled out a spray bottle from his apron's pocket. "Would you mind standing up?"

Amani got up from her seat, albeit hesitantly.

"Ready?" Kenta asked. Amani nodded. Then, he sprayed a fine mist above her head, allowing the light, floral scent to settle on her.

"Oh wow," she whispered.

"The full treatment, remember?" he said with a smile. "Thanks for coming in on a weeknight like this. We really appreciate it."

Suddenly, they heard a pan crash from the kitchen. A few moments later, Mia's head popped out through the kitchen door. "We're fine." With that, she was gone again.

"Man, you guys are a bunch of characters," Amani laughed.

"They really are the best. They've helped me more than they know." Kenta looked over at the kitchen door in appreciation.

"So, what's Rowan's story?" Amani asked. "He's just met me, and yet he's going so far out of his way for me."

"That's just how he is," Kenta said with a shrug. "He seems to really care about other people and wants to make them happy. And not just in the moment. Long-term happy."

"Why?"

Kenta stared thoughtfully at the kitchen door. "I'm still figuring that out," he replied.

As the night continued, Amani couldn't keep a smile off her face. At one point, Rowan even had her on her feet, spinning her around the empty restaurant as she laughed away. "Watch out, Amani. Rowan will have you up dancing all night long if he gets the chance!" Mia yelled from the kitchen doorway.

A wall of anxiety hit Amani as she realized she was once again the center of attention. Letting go of Rowan's hand, she quickly sat back down in her booth.

Rowan joined her. "Everything okay?"

"Just feeling a little overwhelmed. I can't remember the last time I've been pampered like this."

"Mmm. When we've avoided something like this for so long, it takes some time to get used to it."

"I didn't realize how hard it had become to take care of myself," she murmured. At this, Amani started tearing up. She could feel how this evening had begun to refill her nearly empty well; a well that hadn't been replenished in a very long time.

"Well, let's not stop now, huh?" Rowan said with a smile.

Throughout the rest of the evening, Amani was bombarded with positive experiences that were all centered around her. Each one reinforced that it was okay for her to enjoy herself and be the center of attention—that no one was going to be upset with her for being the recipient of this dedicated energy and time. She could simply be, and not serve, and that became more and more okay.

At the end of the evening, as the four sat eating crème brulée, Amani couldn't express her gratitude enough. Through glossy eyes, she said, "I've never experienced anything like that before. Thank you so, so much for the food, the conversation, the chance to open up—everything."

Kenta, Mia, and Rowan smiled. "Our pleasure," Rowan said.

"Please, let me help clean up." Amani used her spoon to gesture at the plates on the table. "It's the least I can do."

Rowan shook his head. "Not a chance. I needed a taste tester, and who did I meet? Someone who seemed like they could really benefit from being nurtured. So really, this night was a win-win for me."

Amani inhaled slowly, as if to breathe in those words. "Nurtured." That concept had been so foreign to her for so long. But as Amani took the last bite of this delicious dessert, she accepted that she didn't have to worry about cleaning up the dishes. She didn't have to tidy up the table. She didn't have to do *anything*.

And while that idea would have skyrocketed her anxiety in the past, it didn't right now.

Right now, she was content—even happy—to be taken care of.

A MOMENT IN THE MIRROR: NEGLECTING ONESELF

As you consider your own life, can you recognize Amani's False Belonging Habit: **I believe if I put others' needs and expectations above my own, I will belong.**

Giving to others is a wonderful thing to do. The world needs kind and generous souls! However, a person like Amani tends to overdo generous giving to the point of imbalance, where her own wants and needs disappear into the background and she depletes herself to serve others.

When we've been putting ourselves at the bottom of our priorities for so long, it can be jarring to try and move ourselves up that list. We might experience feelings of guilt or even worry we've lost our purpose. As we work through this process, it's important to know that we're not letting go of our giving nature altogether. Instead, we're simply looking to find the balance between giving and receiving. We're looking to find a truer sense of belonging outside our False Belonging Habit.

To determine if this Habit applies to you, listen deeply to yourself as you ask yourself the following questions. Focus on curiosity and self-reflection without shame or judgment.

1. Can you name the last time you did something just for you?
2. How do you feel when you think about asking for help? Is it hard?
3. Do you change the topic when the attention is focused on you?
4. Do you quickly dismiss people's efforts to attend to you?
5. When someone agrees to do a task, but it doesn't get done, how often do you just handle it yourself?

6. Do you hesitate to tell a friend you're struggling, because you would be asking them to spend emotional energy on you?

Amani's False Belonging Habit leads to her neglecting herself. Now let's meet Mia and see how her Habit manifests.

CHAPTER 4

MIA: PUSHING LOVE AWAY

"Mia, can you grab the cinnamon please?" Mia's grandmother asked from across the kitchen.

Mia complied, her eyes glued to her phone.

"What's so important on that?" her grandma teased, adding the spice to the bowl.

"Just talking to a friend."

"Well," her grandma said, walking over to envelop her in a big hug. "They'll still be there after we're done frying the batter."

Mia finally looked up and smirked. "Okay, okay." She squirmed out of her grandma's embrace and peered at the bowl of batter. Grandma had finally agreed to teach Mia how to make buñuelos, using a family recipe that she'd kept secret until now. It was Mia's favorite treat, and she was excited to be able to make them whenever she wanted.

"Do you think Mom will like them?"

"I think so," her grandmother said. But there was a tone in her voice, a little hesitation, that Mia knew all too well.

"Mom *is* coming, right? She promised. I haven't seen her in months."

Her grandmother let out a deep sigh. "Mia—"

"No, she isn't. Because she canceled. Again." Mia's hands were suddenly clammy from the hot anger bubbling within her. "What's the excuse this time? Flat tire? A cold? Got an invite to something more exciting?"

"Let's forget about her, hmm?" her grandmother said, resting her hand on Mia's arm. "Abuelo's out on the porch. After we finish up here, we can go enjoy the sunshine with him."

Mia could see the pleading in her grandmother's eyes, but the pain was building inside her. If Mia didn't do something, she felt like she was going to explode.

"I have to go to the bathroom," Mia said.

Mia walked past the downstairs bathroom and climbed the steps to the second-floor one to put more physical space between her and her grandma. Her body was nearly shaking from rage; she could feel that it was about to boil over. She needed to do something to release it. She hopped into the shower, threw her shampoo bottle on the tile floor, and stomped on it over and over until it burst. As she watched the gooey contents ooze out of the nozzle, she desperately hoped to feel better.

But that relief never came.

Mia closed her eyes and took a few shaky breaths. She could hear her grandmother calling for her. She should go back, but the thought of it made her heart ache. *What if Abuela leaves me too?*

Instead, Mia ignored her grandmother and hurried to her room. She grabbed her headphones off her nightstand and turned up her music as loud as her ears could handle.

Mia's False Belonging Habit: I believe if I prevent myself from getting too close, I will be safe emotionally, and then I can belong.

Can you relate? How often do you push someone you love away because you feel caught in your own pain?

THE FEAR OF GETTING TOO CLOSE

A few years later

"How much of that soup is left?" Rowan asked Mia. It was a busy night at The Hearth, and the two were working up a sweat preparing all the meals. Mia wiped her brow with her forearm, her sleeve lifting to reveal the lower half of a tattoo sleeve.

"About a quarter. Want me to start on some more?" Mia asked.

"Yeah, that'd be great. Thanks!"

"Have I told you this is Syd's favorite? I kept a little aside for her, so if you see a teal container in the fridge, don't touch it," Mia instructed her boss, adding stock to a pan.

"Yes, ma'am!" Rowan laughed. "I can't wait to see her for bowling tomorrow. It's been a while. How's she doing?"

"She's good," Mia said. "Just pretty stressed with work and school and everything right now."

"Well, you are about to be seniors. Makes sense," Rowan said, flipping a pan full of onions.

Mia shook her head. "I keep forgetting that. It's wild how fast it's all flown by. I mean we've been together for almost three years now."

Rowan looked up in surprise. "Wow! Getting pretty serious then."

Mia's jaw clenched. She didn't like to think about how serious it was getting. Serious meant more commitment, and more commitment meant it was going to hurt even more when it fell apart.

"Well, you know, we're still in college, so not *that* serious," Mia said, adjusting the headband atop her dark hair.

"What are you talking about, 'not that serious'?" Kenta asked, standing inside the door frame eating the last few bites of an apple as he came back from his break. "You were telling me the other day how I need to go out and find someone who loves me for me, like Syd does for you. That sounds pretty serious to me."

Mia let out a frustrated sigh. "I was just giving you advice. Don't read into *my* side of it too much."

"Hmm," Rowan said. "Well, it is pretty special to find someone who loves you for you. Sometimes it's hard to see that while you're in the thick of it."

Mia shot Rowan a look. "We're not breaking up or anything. I'm just... not rushing things." Mia's annoyance was growing by the second. "Can we just talk about something else?" She said, more of an order than a request.

"Kenta, can you prep some more salads, please?" Rowan asked.

Kenta opened his mouth to make one more comment, but Mia shot him a look that made him reconsider. "Can do," he said cheerfully, and turned toward the walk-in to get started on the salads.

"Ah! Just to the left!" Mia said as Rowan's bowling ball veered at the last moment.

"I swear, if there were only nine pins, I'd be great at this game," Rowan joked.

"At least you got nine! I'm stuck getting four or five over here," Sydney said, her long earrings clanging as she laughed.

Rowan had been bowling with Mia since she was a kid, but Sydney was a newbie at the sport.

"And another miss," Sydney snickered as her ball rolled into the gutter. She sat next to Rowan. "If I wasn't so busy, part of me would want to come down here and practice so I'm not so bad next time."

"Hey, you don't have to be good at everything," Rowan reassured her. "How's your schedule looking with classes starting back up soon?"

Before she could answer, Mia knocked down eight pins. "Atta way!" Rowan cheered.

"Well, hold off on that until we see what happens with the last two," Mia said.

Sydney answered while clapping. "It's been pretty hectic. The worst part is, I live so far away from campus and work. The commute just makes the day so much longer."

"Have you thought about moving closer?" Rowan asked, getting up for his turn.

"Actually, um…"

"You didn't tell me you're thinking of moving," Mia said, sitting down next to Sydney. "Is that true?"

"I was actually gonna bring this up to you later, but… what if we moved in together? Closer to campus?" Sydney asked.

Mia could see the excitement mixed with nerves in Sydney's eyes. But the only thing Mia felt was pure panic.

"And *that's* how it's done!" Rowan exclaimed after getting a strike. He turned around, clearly expecting applause, but was met with palpable tension instead. "Did I miss something?"

"Just, um, talking about potential moving options," Sydney said.

"Mmm hmm. Yeah, I think it's good to, um, not rush the decision. It's pretty big. Don't want to mess up a good thing. Your current apartment, I mean," Mia sputtered. "You're up, Syd."

Mia could see how much Sydney was trying to hide her disappointment, but it still shone through.

The rest of the game was tense. Sydney and Rowan tried to lighten the mood, but Mia found herself withdrawing from the conversation. She tried to be polite and not ruin the evening, but mostly she just wanted to be alone.

When the trio were returning their shoes to the counter, Rowan piped up, "All right! Where do you want to go to dinner?"

"Thai sounds pretty good! Or there's that pizza place down the street," Sydney offered.

"Actually, you know, I think that pretzel isn't sitting well with me," Mia cut in. "My stomach is pretty messed up. I might just call it and go home."

"Oh no, I didn't realize." Rowan said.

Mia shook her head dismissively. "You two feel free to grab something. I'll talk to you later," she said, giving Syd a kiss on the cheek before quickly walking out.

"Great," Sydney sighed, massaging her hands over her eyes.

"How are you feeling?" Rowan asked.

"I just… she gives such mixed signals, you know? One minute she seems super into us and so happy, but then she does this and freaks out and can't even have a conversation about moving in. I just don't get it. Maybe she doesn't want to be together after all."

Rowan inhaled slowly, seeming to collect his thoughts. "I've noticed that sometimes it's the opposite. When someone really cares about a person, that's often when they push back the most. Deep love can be scary."

Sydney took her own deep breath. "I know she had some stuff go down, with her mom not being around. I wish I knew how to help her with that, because I really want her to feel safe with me, you know? I'd never leave her like that."

Rowan gave her a reassuring smile. "I think, on some level, she realizes that. In all the years I've known Mia, I've never seen her open up with anyone the way she does with you."

Sydney looked down. "I know, I know. And I don't want to push her too far and lose her. If I did… I don't know what I'd do, honestly. So I guess I'll just wait as long as I need to. She's worth that."

"She really is, isn't she? She's something special," Rowan said. The two of them stood in silence for a moment, nodding as they felt the truth of that statement.

Rowan clapped his hands together. "Well, let's not have you wait on an empty stomach. Thai or pizza? Your choice, my treat."

Sydney cracked a smile. "Thai please."

LEARNING TO SEND LOVE INTO THE WORLD

Several days later, a groggy Mia stumbled out of her grandparents' house to meet an all-too-chipper Rowan. "I don't know if I would've agreed to this if I knew how early you wanted to leave," she said.

"How'd you sleep?" Rowan asked, climbing onto his bike.

"Ugh."

"Yeah, you have a lot on your mind."

Mia grumbled as she walked to the garage to retrieve her bike. Her mind flashed back to Sydney, whom she hadn't heard from since the bowling alley. Of course, Mia hadn't reached out to her either. She really didn't want to talk about the whole moving thing, so she'd decided it was best to avoid the situation altogether until Sydney reached out.

"Let's hit the road!" Rowan announced. "The fresh air will do you some good. Wanna stop at the farmer's market? It's about a mile ahead."

"Sure."

Soon, they were moving along the bike path at a leisurely pace. Rowan was right: the fresh air did feel good, though Mia didn't want to admit it.

Before long, they reached the farmer's market. They parked their bikes and walked down the center aisle. "Tonya!" Rowan called to a woman minding one of the stalls. "That finicky orchid of mine? It finally has a flower!"

Rowan peeled away to continue the conversation; Mia kept her distance, still not in the mood to mingle after her experience at the bowling alley. Rowan soon rejoined her.

"If you ever need plant advice, talk to Tonya. She's the best," Rowan said.

"Well, with my black thumb, it's probably best that I avoid plants entirely," Mia quipped.

Rowan chuckled as they approached a stall with a woman selling locally harvested honey. She was talking to three different customers at once: "Ooh, it's your lucky day! That's the last one!" "I tell ya, this honeycomb is just going to change your life!" "Your perfume is just amazing! Where did you get it?" Even Mia couldn't help but smile at this woman's infectious enthusiasm.

When it was Rowan's turn, he was smiling widely. "You are just a ball of light! You're making every person's day a little better when they talk to you."

The woman smiled back. "You need to stop before you make me blush!"

"If blushing helps you see how amazing you are, then blush away!"

"Wow. Thank you," she said, clearly touched by Rowan's sincerity.

After Rowan bought a jar of orange blossom honey, Mia watched the woman talk to the next customer. Somehow, her smile was even bigger.

"That was nice, what you said to that lady," Mia said as they walked back to their bicycles.

"Well, I think everyone deserves to have their true selves seen. Even if it's by a stranger."

They rode another several miles in silence, and Mia was finally starting to relax into the gentle pace of her pedaling. Just as she was starting to get into a rhythm, Rowan started slowing down ahead of her.

"I think this is a good spot for a break," he said. They stopped right next to a bench with an elderly woman sitting on it. "Mind if we join you?" Rowan asked the woman.

"Not at all," she replied. She was looking across the grass at a few squirrels.

"How is your day going?" Rowan asked her as he dismounted.

Looking a bit surprised, the woman turned toward him. "Oh, it's just fine. Yours?"

Mia stayed back a little, still balancing on her bike. She knew Rowan would get this woman chatting, and she didn't feel like taking part.

"Oh, we've been having a lovely day..." Rowan started talking about the market as he sat down next to her. Then he asked, "What have you been up to today?"

"Well, this is the highlight. I live just over there, and I came out here for some fresh air. I don't do much else these days."

Mia noticed the woman's shoulders drooping as she spoke.

"Wow. The way you described that sounds very lonely," Rowan said.

After a moment, the woman whispered, "It is."

Mia felt her body tense. She knew that lonely feeling all too well. Sure, she tried to put on a tough face, to not let anyone know that the void in her heart was sometimes so enormous that she worried it might swallow her whole. But some days, that loneliness could be all-consuming.

Come to think of it, though, she hadn't felt that intense loneliness in a while. Not since she met Sydney, in fact.

Mia snapped back into the present as the woman began telling Rowan that her husband had passed away two years ago, and her daughter lives in another state. Now Mia's shoulders sank. That must be so hard, to lose someone you've been with for so long. Even losing Syd, whom she'd only known for three years, would devastate Mia.

That thought sent Mia down a rabbit hole. What if something

did happen to Syd? What if something happened to her tomorrow, and the last thing Mia had said to her was that bogus excuse about having a stomachache?

Sydney deserved more than that. And Mia wanted to be the one to tell her.

Mia watched as Rowan listened intently to the woman's stories. He was so enthralled, paying such close attention to this woman who clearly needed an empathetic ear, that he even started to get choked up. Mia knew he didn't mind. She could feel the connection between the two of them.

When Rowan did speak, he asked questions. "What's one of your favorite memories with your husband?"

"When we were young, we'd go dancing almost every weekend. Not like what you kids do now," she motioned at Mia, "but proper dances with steps and routines. My favorite was the mambo," she said, a smile growing on her face. "Hank would whip me around faster than anyone else on the dance floor!"

"When was the last time you went dancing?"

"Oh, a long time ago, before Hank got sick. I don't think my old bones could do much anymore."

Rowan shook his head. "Uh-uh, I don't buy it. The woman that tore up the dance floor? She's still in there, I promise you. I'm guessing if I could call up Hank right now, he'd tell me the same thing. And I doubt he'd want the highlight of your day to be sitting alone on this park bench."

The woman sighed in agreement.

Rowan got up, but he paused before getting on his bike. "How do you mambo again? Like this?" Rowan started swinging his hips and legs in a manner that vaguely resembled dancing.

The woman laughed. "No, not quite. You have to step to the side more."

"Like this?" Rowan's hips were still gyrating at an odd angle.

"You look like you're having a spasm," Mia said with a chuckle.

"Almost," the woman said, pushing against the armrest and slowly getting up. "More like this." The woman carefully moved her feet and twisted her hips.

"Aye! *Avive la Vie*! Look at you go!" Rowan cheered.

A wide smile spread across the woman's face as Rowan tried to copy her steps. "That's it!" she said.

"Fun! Thanks!" Rowen delighted.

The two exchanged warm goodbyes. As Mia and Rowan began riding away down the paved path, Mia glanced back at the woman one last time. Her whole energy had changed.

"How do you do that?" Mia asked Rowan.

"Do what?"

"You're like, best friends with this lady you just met. I could never."

Rowan slowed down so he was beside Mia. "Well, I guess I don't view love as being reserved to only a few select people. I just put it out into the world and see what comes back."

"But what if you give someone love and they let you down?" she asked quietly.

"They might. I mean, that woman back there could have shooed me away when I started asking about her life. But in my experience, more often than not, the opposite happens. Remember when we first met? You were, what, eight or nine? And you wanted *nothing* to do with me."

Mia nodded. "You were so bubbly it was alarming."

Rowan let out a belly laugh. "But I didn't stop there, did I? I was good friends with your grandparents, so I kept coming by and putting myself out there. And look where we are now!"

"You're pretty brave to do that." Mia had meant this to be a joke, but it came out quite sincere instead. Because in her bones, Mia really meant it.

"Yeah, well, it's not just me. We all have the courage to do it; we just have to be willing to take that leap of faith." Rowan picked up his pace as he led them around a curve.

Mia contemplated that idea. Had she ever really taken a leap of faith? Not with strangers, that's for sure. But even with friends, she rarely truly opened up to someone.

As they rode, she thought again about that distant loneliness that had plagued her for so long; how Sydney had helped chase it away; the fear of something happening to Sydney; the newfound courage to tell Syd how important she is to her.

How tired she was of being afraid to let people in.

She slowed down and pulled off the path. "I'll catch up!" she yelled ahead to Rowan. She pulled out her phone, channeled that buried courage, and texted Sydney about meeting up that evening.

DROPPING ONE'S ARMOR

"Hey babe!" Sydney said as she hopped in the passenger seat, leaning over to give Mia a kiss.

"Hey," Mia responded quietly.

"So, what do you have in mind for tonight? We never really do 'date night'," Sydney said, making air quotes with her fingers, "so I'm really curious what you…"

"Before we go into that, can I… can I just get something off my chest?" Mia was fiddling with her key ring, unable to make eye contact with Sydney.

"Uh, sure?"

Breathing in through her nose like Rowan had taught her, Mia tried to steady her breath. "Um, I wanted to say I'm sorry for how I acted, when you brought up moving in together."

Sydney cut in, "Oh, that was on me! I didn't mean to spring it on you. I should have known better than to bring that up out of the blue."

Now Mia's eyes shot to Sydney's. "But I don't want you to think that you can't bring up things like moving in together. I *want* to have those conversations. It's just… hard for me."

"I know," Syd whispered, taking Mia's hand in hers.

"This is, um, really weird for me. Being vulnerable and all," Mia said with an uneasy laugh. "I mean, I used to. When I was younger. I was apparently very in touch with my *feelings*," Mia said, wiggling her fingers at the foreign word. "But I just remember getting my hopes up when Abuela would say that Mom was coming to visit. I'd brush my hair, draw her a picture, get all ready, and then Abuela would come upstairs and say that something came up, and she couldn't make it. That happened *so* many times, Syd."

Mia took her hand away and rubbed her face.

"When you get burned that much, you learn not to get close to the flame anymore. Or, I guess, let the flame get close to you." Mia could feel her eyes starting to water. She held her breath, not sure if she could continue.

"I get it," Sydney said.

"And I think that's what I've been most afraid of, why I was scared to talk about living together. Because what if we move in, and then I freak out and totally pull back? Then that's going to scare you, and maybe you'll regret the move and question being with me and…"

Sydney grabbed Mia's hands, holding them both tightly. "Hey, I know it's not going to be perfect. Life isn't perfect. But just knowing that you're willing to talk about it makes all the difference."

Mia nodded. "Well, even if I'm scared—which, I am," Mia said, letting out another uneasy laugh, "I want to be more open for you."

Sydney smiled softly. "For *us*."

Mia turned to Sydney and, seeing her partner's eyes full of empathy and love, finally felt like she could breathe again. "I love you."

Sydney squeezed Mia's hands. "I love you, too."

Relief washed over Mia, and a wide smile spread across her face. "Cool."

"Cool," Sydney reiterated with a big grin.

"Well," Mia said, shifting back into a driving position. "Guess we can get going then."

"And where exactly are we going again?" Sydney asked, buckling up.

Mia's eyes danced with mischief as she glanced over at her partner. "It's a surprise."

With a laugh, Sydney said, "Good thing I trust you."

Mia breathed in those words and drove off.

A MOMENT IN THE MIRROR: PUSHING LOVE AWAY

Within yourself, can you recognize Mia's False Belonging Habit: **I believe if I prevent myself from getting too close, I will be safe emotionally, and then I can belong.**

Most of us can relate to protecting our heart at one point or another. After our first breakup, we may have been cautious when letting our next love in. Sometimes, setting boundaries with callous or untrustworthy people is what we need for our emotional and mental health, and the feeling of safety it provides allows us to re-enter the world. But when those boundaries harden into impenetrable walls, we begin to exclude everyone from getting close, including those who could add joy and love to our lives.

It can be difficult to work up the nerve to finally allow others in after shielding yourself away for so long. So before making any big moves, let's start with seeing if you identify with this Habit.

1. Do you frequently put your guard up and get defensive?
2. Do you worry about what others think of you? Do you have the tendency to assume that you're being rejected?
3. Do you find yourself walking off during arguments saying, "I can't talk about this right now!" and even refuse to speak about it later?
4. Do you isolate yourself when you don't feel safe?
5. Do you experience a sense of emptiness or hopelessness without being able to put a name to what you're feeling?
6. Can you relate to having this fear of intimacy with someone, like Mia does with Sydney?

We've now gone through the first three False Belonging Habits. Next, let's meet Tate and see how his False Belonging Habit affects his life.

CHAPTER 5

TATE: GETTING LOST IN ANXIETY

Tate sat in his truck, constantly scanning the parking lot. His pale skin was starting to turn pink from the sun beating through the windshield.

An email popped up on his phone with the subject line "Mom/ Dad Final Will & Testament." As he started to read the document from his brother, Molly's SUV pulled up next to him.

Tate hopped out so quickly that his baseball hat hit the top of the car door. "Hi girls!" he said, quickly adjusting it. His two daughters came and gave him a big hug. Molly hung behind, coming around her car to lean against the passenger door.

"Why don't you two hop in the truck? I've got to talk to Mom about something," Tate said.

"What is it?" Molly asked, clearly annoyed. "I can see you're all worked up about something."

Tate reached into his pocket and unfolded a spreadsheet, highlighted in multiple colors.

"Not the damn spreadsheet," Molly grumbled.

"Did you spend over $400 on a phone this week?" Tate asked, pointing at a line on the sheet. "I have the charge right here."

"Yes, I did. For Nadia. She dropped hers, and the screen shattered. And it's not a new phone—it's a refurbished one."

"Well, I would have liked to have at least been clued in. That's a lot of money."

Molly sighed. "Remember, we agreed that if it's less than $500, we don't need to discuss it."

"Well, I mean, four hundred and..." Tate peered at the paper. "Four hundred and sixty-four dollars is pretty close to five hundred, I'd say."

"Tate, I looked at our budget for the month. We're *fine*." Tate could hear the irritation growing in his wife's voice.

"I know, but there were other charges too. Some new shoes, the most expensive car wash..." He trailed off as a dent on the front bumper of Molly's SUV caught his eye. "What happened here?"

"I hit a raccoon."

"So now we have to pay to get this fixed, too?" he huffed.

"I showed it to Dad, and he said it shouldn't be too much actually."

"And you know they're going to try to upcharge you, too. It's always more expensive than you think it's going to be. That's how they get you. And then they'll say there's something else wrong..."

"Did you not just hear what I said?" Molly's voice was sharp. "It's going to be cheap. If you could just *listen* to me instead of being so damn wound up in your head about all the awful things that could happen, maybe we wouldn't be... like this." She waved her hand back and forth between them.

"Like what?"

"THIS, Tate! Separated! Trying to figure out if we're going to save this godforsaken marriage!"

Tate clenched his jaw, inspecting the dent again so he didn't have to look at Molly. "*If*, huh?"

"Sure, *now* you listen," she said, rolling her eyes.

Tate returned to stand across from Molly. "I don't choose to be like this, you know."

Molly's anger finally dissipated, and now her eyes were filled with something else: defeat. "I know. But you also don't try not to."

They locked eyes for a few moments longer, and then Molly sighed again. "Anyway, I've got to run. Remember, Ellie needs help with her math homework tonight." She opened the back door to Tate's truck and said goodbye to her daughters, then got into her car and drove off.

As Tate climbed back into his truck, he found himself obsessing over Molly's departure. Where did she have to hurry off to? Was she going to meet up with their friends? Tell them all what a neurotic jerk he is?

"Daddy!" his youngest, Ellie, called from the backseat. "Can we get ice cream?"

Tate was so lost in thought that he barely registered the request. "Maybe later," he said, not even turning to look at his girls, whom he hadn't seen all week. "Right now, Daddy has to take care of some stuff back at home."

Sensing their father's mood, the girls stayed quiet for the drive home.

Tate's False Belonging Habit: I believe if I anticipate bad outcomes and try to prevent them, I will prove I'm responsible, and I will belong.

Can you relate? How often does your anxiety keep you from being truly present?

THE FEAR-BUILDING
CYCLE OF ANXIETY

Tate was still fired up from his conversation with Molly when he and his daughters sat down to dinner. As Tate plopped the bag holding their meals onto the small kitchen table, his daughters saw their chance to start talking about their days.

"At lunch, Will tried to balance his apple juice on his head, and it went all down his face!" Nadia laughed, looking to see her father's reaction. "Isn't that funny, Dad?"

"Huh? Oh, yeah, very funny," he responded flatly. Should he call Molly? Try to get a better answer about her spending?

"What if we tried that?" Ellie asked with a cheeky smile.

"But instead of just one, *two* cups!" Nadia chimed in.

Usually, the idea of cleaning up the mess would drive Tate wild, and the girls knew it. But his mind was still elsewhere. "Uh, yeah. Sure."

Tate's daughters exchanged looks. The girls quickly ate up the rest of their takeout in a defeated silence, then excused themselves to go watch TV.

Tate went to throw away the containers and stubbed his toe on the side of the island. Swearing under his breath, he leaned against the counter for support. He still wasn't used to this small apartment layout. His mind wandered to his home's large kitchen, which he knew like the back of his hand. He'd never stubbed his toe there.

Feeling frustrated and rather hopeless, he tried to turn it around and encourage himself. *You'll work things out*, he told himself without much conviction.

Tate hurried past his daughters and into his pseudo-office, which was a desk in the girls' bedroom. When he was stressed, there was always one thing that could distract him: accounting. Numbers couldn't lie or let you down. Numbers only spoke the truth.

As he was looking through his expenses, he noticed a high charge on his wife's credit card to a "Brown & Brown." Was that a law firm? Was she looking into divorce papers? They had promised that they weren't at that point yet, that they were going to give each other some time to see if they could resolve things.

Tate grabbed a stick of gum and started aggressively chewing it as he thought through all the awful scenarios.

Suddenly, a small voice said, "Dad, it's time for us to go to bed." He nearly jumped at Ellie's voice. "What?" He looked down at his watch and instantly scolded himself. The girls should have been in bed forty-five minutes ago. When he saw his daughter carrying her textbooks, he silently cursed himself again. "Do you still need help with your math homework, Ellie?"

"No, I'm good," she mumbled.

"Come on in. I'll take my laptop out." The girls shuffled in, and Tate said his goodnights and gently closed the door behind him. He leaned against it a moment, his eyes closed. He'd wasted one of his precious nights with his daughters—and for what?

Molly's comment rang in his head. *If you weren't so wound up in your head, maybe we wouldn't be like this...*

By the time Tate went to lie down, his body was exhausted, yet his mind wouldn't stop repeating awful possibility after awful possibility. It took hours until he finally drifted off to an equally unrestful sleep, where his dreams provided little respite from the stress.

FEARING THE WORST BRINGS OUT THE WORST

Exhausted from his poor night's sleep, Tate parked in the lot for his next delivery. He tipped his head back, allowing his eyelids to close for just a few moments.

He was awoken by a tap on the driver's side window. Tate stepped out of the truck to grab a box of produce out of the back.

"Rough night?" Mia asked.

"When you get to be my age, every night is rough," he joked, not letting on how rough it really was. Over his years of making deliveries, Tate had come to enjoy his stops at The Hearth. These were good people. He even took his family to eat here regularly—or at least, he did when they were still living under one roof.

He walked into the kitchen to find Rowan on the phone. "You're sure you can't deliver it? The table won't fit in my car."

Tate listened as it became apparent that the table Rowan was expecting wasn't going to be showing up.

Rowan hung up, sighed, then turned to Tate with a smile. "Every day is a gift, isn't it?"

Tate laughed. "You need help picking something up? You're my last delivery. I could grab it if it's not too far." This was the kind of guy Tate prided himself on being—maybe not the warmest or chattiest, but he was always willing to help out someone who needed it.

"Really? That'd be amazing," Rowan said. "It's only about ten minutes away. I'll come to help you lift it in the truck."

"I'll hold down the fort," Mia chimed in from behind the baking rack.

Soon, Tate and Rowan were on the road, chatting and catching up. Suddenly, Tate cut off the conversation and leaned forward to get a better view out the windshield. "Wait, I think... That's Rick!"

The car passed, and Tate sat back in his seat. "That was my brother," he said incredulously. "I... I can't believe he came to town and didn't tell me."

"Maybe it's a surprise for you," Rowan suggested warmly.

But Tate could barely speak anymore. With each moment that passed, a new feeling arose seemingly out of nowhere: hurt, betrayal, anger. Then, a disturbing thought rose up.

Last month we had a few conversations about Dad's will. He just emailed me about it, actually. Is he here to work on it? Is that why he didn't tell me? But Mom would have told me if Rick was coming to visit, wouldn't she? But obviously she didn't. So, it's something secretive enough that they even got Mom to hide it from me. But that's not that surprising, honestly. She always favored Rick. She'd blow up on me about any little thing, even if it wasn't my fault...

Tate's internal temperature was shooting up. His heartbeat quickened as he imagined each new possible betrayal.

"Are you okay?" Rowan asked. His voice startled Tate, who'd nearly forgotten he was there.

"I'm just surprised," he responded. "And I've seen how things like this can break up families, and..."

"Maybe you should give him a call?" Rowan suggested.

Tate waved dismissively. "He'd probably make up some story..."

"Isn't that what you're doing now, though? Making up a story of why he's in town?" Rowan's voice was calm and even, but Tate felt like he'd slapped him across the face.

"Geez, way to call me out!"

"I didn't mean it as an insult. Just an observation," Rowan said, seemingly unbothered by the growing tension in the cab of the truck.

"Let's just get your table," Tate mumbled.

For the rest of the drive, Tate didn't bother making small talk. He kept flipping between being upset with Rowan for not even attempting to sympathize with him, and feeling hopeless about his relationship with his brother and mom. They picked up the table and returned it to The Hearth with hardly a word passing between them.

As Tate started his truck to head home, his phone rang. It was Molly.

"Hello?"

"Hey, I just wanted to make sure you're picking up the girls from dance today," Molly said.

"Yeah, at five, right?" Tate confirmed.

As he said this, he could hear a faint male voice in the background say, "I'll meet you inside."

Tate clenched the steering wheel. He tried to hide the suspicion from his voice as he asked, "So what are you up to tonight?"

"Oh, nothing. Just wanted to make sure they wouldn't be stranded. I'll talk to you later."

"Yeah, talk later. Bye," Tate said.

Tate's mind went into full panic mode. Had she met someone else? Or was that the divorce lawyer he had seen in the credit card charges? He sat in The Hearth's parking lot, too anxious to do anything but stare out the windshield.

Tate finally broke his trance when he saw a figure moving. It was Rowan, taking a trash bag out to the dumpster. Rowan noticed Tate was still there, waved, and headed back inside. As he left, his comment from earlier rang in Tate's head: *Aren't you making up a story?*

Just then, another memory surfaced: an argument he'd had with Molly when they were still living together. "That's not even true, Tate!" she'd told him after he'd accused her of... something. He couldn't remember what. "You're so in your head it's like you're not even here!"

He started thinking about how often this happened to him: when he couldn't listen to the girls talk about their days at school because he was agitated about something, when he ran away to his office to solve work problems instead of spending quality time with his wife... there were so many.

Tate started overheating, so he cranked up his A/C. With his face inches from the vent, he tried to push out these memories. But they kept coming. He didn't know what was happening, but he was beginning to see how miserable his lack of trust was making his life.

One thing was clear: Tate owed Rowan an apology. So, he swallowed his pride, hopped out of the truck, and knocked on the back door of the restaurant.

"Oh!" Rowan said, surprised. "Did you forget something?"

"No, not that. I..." This was more uncomfortable than Tate had expected. "Sorry for, you know, all that in the truck."

"All what?" Rowan asked.

"I get a little stressed sometimes. Always thinking the worst thing. It's not my best quality." Tate didn't know where to look, so he kept his eyes fixated on the clock behind Rowan. Talking about this felt strange, unnatural even. Rowan was one of the few people to call him out on making up stories, though, so Tate felt the need to explain himself.

Rowan listened intently, giving his full attention to Tate. "That can start to take its toll after a while, huh?"

"You're telling me," Tate agreed. "It's just like, how did I get to this point, you know? The uptight guy who thinks the world is out to get him—that's not who I thought I'd turn out to be."

"Who *did* you think you'd be?" Rowan asked.

Tate went to answer, then hesitated. "I can't even remember anymore. I guess a good dad. A good husband. A good person."

"Can't you be uptight and still a good person?"

Tate finally cracked a smile. "Touché. I'm not *bad*, I know that. I could just benefit from a few improvements."

"I like the word 'growth' more," Rowan said.

Growth. Tate liked the sound of that. He didn't have to fix himself; he just had to work on growing.

CONFRONTING ONE'S RESTLESS ANXIETY

Tate fidgeted on his mat, smoothing the thinning hair underneath his baseball hat. Was he wearing the right thing? He had never been to a yoga class; had never *wanted* to go to a yoga class before. But Tate was still feeling a little guilty about how he had acted with Rowan, so when Rowan invited Tate to the class, he agreed to join. Maybe some of Rowan's serenity would rub off on him.

"This is going to be great for you," Rowan said quietly.

A familiar laugh caught Tate's attention. He did a quick look around the room and froze. Molly was in the front row, laughing with the man next to her.

"Shit!" Tate muttered, turning around quickly.

"What is it?" Rowan asked.

"Molly's here," Tate whispered, motioning toward her with his head.

"Oh, wonderful! Sometimes she can't make it on Wednesdays."

"You knew she came here?" Tate hissed, keeping his voice low.

"Of course. You didn't know where she went to yoga?" Rowan asked.

Tate shrugged. "I knew she did yoga sometimes. She probably just started coming here."

"No, she's been a regular here for years."

Tate ignored this point and grabbed his shoes. "I'm leaving." He walked out the door, sneakers in hand.

Rowan followed. "Why run? Why not just take the class? You were going to before you knew she was there."

"I don't want to ruin the class for her." Tate flexed his feet, uncomfortable with his socks touching the sidewalk.

"Why would you?"

"I just would."

"I really don't think she would mind…" Rowan started.

"Look, I don't want to risk doing anything else to mess up our marriage, okay?"

Rowan paused for a moment. "And you think going to this yoga class would do that?"

Tate started going down the rabbit hole. "Maybe! I'm on thin ice already! It's all my fault, this separation. I'm a terrible husband. I'm not present around her or the girls. I'm always caught up in how worried I am about the business or money…"

Rowan cut in. "I can feel your anxiety from here, my friend." He took a breath. "You know, a lot of people break up because of cheating, right? Well, to me it seems like your mistress was your anxiety."

The oddness of this comment stopped Tate dead in his tracks. "My mistress was… what? What does that even mean?"

"I've seen how much your anxiety affects you, in your work and personal life. Your mistress sure is costing you a lot."

"Why do you keep calling it… Ah! The yoga class looks like it's starting."

"Well, I'm going to go do some yoga. Whether you want to join me or not is really up to you," Rowan said, turning to head inside.

Tate stood on the pavement, shoes still in hand. Was Rowan right? He looked through the window at the back of his beloved wife's head. He desperately wanted to patch things up, to win back the love of his life. And if yoga could be a step toward that, as Rowan suggested, what did he have to lose?

Digging into his courage, Tate turned and headed back into the studio.

⟫⟶ ⟵⟪

After the class, Tate went back to The Hearth with Rowan to grab some breakfast. "Whew! Smells like someone had a good workout," Mia said as the two men walked in.

"Why thank you," Rowan said, taking a bow.

"You should've joined us, Mia," Tate said.

"Ha! Flexibility is not my thing. Now, if you want to shoot hoops sometime, then I'm your gal."

As Rowan started cooking up some bacon, Tate regaled Mia with the story of their session. "I wish I had a picture of her face when she saw me! I've never seen Molly so genuinely shocked," Tate laughed, leaning against the counter. "And I finally got to meet her friend, Xavier. I've heard her talk about him, but I've never gotten the chance to meet him... Oh! Maybe that's who I heard on the phone!"

Rowan and Mia gave Tate an odd look, and he responded with a sheepish smile. "When Molly called yesterday, I heard this guy's voice in the background and I, uh, got a little carried away wondering who it might be."

"That tracks," Mia said.

"What's that mean?"

"You just tend to get worked up about things is all," she said.

Rather than jump to anger, like he normally did, Tate accepted the remark. Maybe that yoga had calmed him more than he realized. "I guess I need to work on that. Especially if I want to win Molly back."

"Well, keep hanging out with this guy and you'll get there," Mia said, motioning to Rowan with her spatula. "I've never met anyone more zen."

Rowan laughed. "Well, I think yoga's a great start. And hey, if Molly sees that you're able to change your view on yoga, maybe she'll see that you can change other things too?"

Tate nodded, really considering the idea. If he committed to this yoga thing, he could actually *show* Molly that he's willing to change rather than continuing to *tell* her over and over.

At the very least, it was worth a shot.

TRADING ANXIETY FOR PRESENCE

Within a few weeks, Tate had developed a new weekend routine. Every Saturday, he'd wake up early to go to yoga with Rowan, then grab breakfast at The Hearth after. Mia was always there, but Tate also met a few other regulars: Kenta, who also worked at The Hearth, and Amani, a social worker in training who stopped by to chat and have a meal when she had a morning to spare.

Soon, Tate found himself being invited to other gatherings with the Crew. He grabbed dinner at a new Peruvian place with Kenta one night. Another evening, he attended a seminar with Amani about incorporating creativity into parenting after she'd been talking it up for weeks. He had lived contently within his comfortable bubble for so long, and until recently these experiences would have been well outside his comfort zone. Yet he was genuinely surprised—and pleased—to find he actually enjoyed them.

Then, about two months after he'd started attending the yoga classes, his shock reached an entirely new level.

"Molly is coming!" Tate announced, bursting through the kitchen door of The Hearth on Saturday morning.

"What?" Kenta asked.

"We were chatting after class, and I told her about coming here, and she asked to come. God, I'm nervous." Tate dabbed at the sweat forming on his brow.

"Well, I'm excited to meet her," Kenta said with a smile.

Tate heard the front door open and rushed out from the kitchen to see if it was Molly. It was Mia. "You've never looked this excited to see me," she joked, rearranging some of the tables.

"Molly's on her way. I don't want to leave her waiting," Tate responded, looking out the window.

"As in your *wife*, Molly?"

Tate locked eyes with Mia. "Don't say anything to offend her, okay? This needs to go well."

Mia put her hands up in innocence. "I only speak the truth, my man. If someone is offended by that, it's not my problem."

Before Tate could argue, there was a light knock on the door. Tate rushed over and opened it.

"Sorry, I didn't know if they were open," Molly said, looking around the dining room. "Ooh, I've never been in here when it was empty!"

"Hi," Mia piped up, jogging over.

"Hello! I'm Molly," she said, looking a little surprised by this young woman in her face.

"I know. I'm Mia. Take a seat wherever." With that, Mia disappeared to the back.

Tate fidgeted with his wedding ring as Molly looked around the room. "She *knows*, huh?" Molly said, more of a statement than a question. "Do you know her well?"

"Yeah, I've been hanging out with Rowan and his friends lately. They're a pretty cool group."

As if on cue, Rowan emerged from the kitchen. "Molly! So glad you could join us. Do you like omelets?"

"I love omelets!"

"Wonderful! They'll be done shortly. Make yourself at home." Rowan headed back to the kitchen, and Mia came back out carrying silverware and plates.

"Is anyone else joining us?" Mia asked as she set the table.

"I don't think so," Tate said, shaking his head.

"Oh. I was wondering if Molly's friend from yoga was coming," Mia said offhandedly.

"My 'friend from yoga'?" Molly asked.

"Yeah, the one that made Tate jealous," Mia said with a snort, heading back to the kitchen.

Tate's anxiety shot up. This was exactly what he didn't want Molly to hear. But as that anxious feeling in his stomach started to build, he thought about what he had been discussing with Rowan—about how his anxiety was the reason his marriage was dissolving. So, Tate took a deep breath and forged ahead.

"Yeah, a while ago when you called, I could hear Xavier in the background." He took another breath. "I overreacted, I guess."

A hint of surprise flickered across Molly's face. "Glad to hear that you're no longer threatened by *my gay friend*," Molly said.

"I know, I know. I'm really trying to not get sucked into the stories I make up."

"First yoga, now this? What have you done with my husband?" Molly joked.

Rather than shrugging it off like Molly expected, Tate looked down, then looked her in the eye. "Well, maybe he's just growing up a little."

Before they could speak another word, Rowan, Kenta, and Mia emerged from the kitchen, each carrying dishes.

"Bon appétit!" Rowan announced, setting the food on the table.

After a quick introduction between Kenta and Molly, the group was happily chatting as they enjoyed the flavorful meal.

"How are the girls?" Rowan asked Molly.

"Yeah, how did that solar system diorama go for Ellie?" Kenta asked. When Molly gave him a puzzled look, Kenta clarified, "Tate was telling us all about it."

Again, Molly looked over at Tate in surprise. "That's, um… sorry, I'm not used to him getting involved with stuff like that." Molly shook herself off. "Other than a few hot glue burns on my fingers, it went well!" she said with a laugh. "She got an A."

Rowan, Kenta, and Mia cheered, "*Avive la vie!*"

The cheer startled Molly, and she laughed again. "Man, I love the energy in here!"

"I always think life is far more exciting with a few cheers now and then," Rowan said with a grin.

The rest of breakfast went swimmingly, and when it was time to leave, Tate offered to walk Molly to her car.

"So chivalrous of you," she joked as they approached her SUV.

Tate was wringing his hands, struggling to find the words for what he wanted to say. "Yeah well, I wanted to tell you how much I'm trying to be different. To not let my worry and stress affect everything. They've been helping with that," he said, nodding toward the restaurant.

"I can see that." Molly said, looking at the door with a faint smile. "I'm not used to you recognizing when you've overreacted, and I love that you're clearly more involved with the girls. But... it's going to take some time on my end. I need to see this isn't just a quick fix."

Tate nodded. "I know. I understand that. I'm realizing how hard it must have been to be with someone who always thinks the worst." Tate released a pent-up breath. "But, yeah, I just wanted to let you know how important you and the girls are to me. And I'm working on it."

She took his hand in hers. "Thank you. That means a lot."

In an instant, the anxiety that had been building inside Tate seemed to float away. All the effort he'd been putting in these past few weeks had been worth it to feel the familiar softness of his wife's hand. "Great." He didn't know what else to say, but he didn't want this moment to end.

"You know... the girls have that sleepover at Lyla's this weekend. Would you wanna come over for dinner on Saturday?"

"Who's cooking?" Tate asked with a smug grin.

"You could grill something, and I'll handle the sides. I'm guessing you've been missing that barbeque," Molly teased.

"Oh, I certainly have," he laughed.

Somehow, the space had closed between them; Tate wasn't sure which of them had moved.

"Saturday then," Molly said, stepping back to pull open her driver's door.

"I'll bring the steaks!" Tate announced. He could hear the boy-like excitement in his voice, and he didn't care.

Saturday couldn't come soon enough.

A MOMENT IN THE MIRROR: GETTING LOST IN ANXIETY

Within yourself, can you recognize Tate's False Belonging Habit: **I believe if I anticipate bad outcomes and try to prevent them, I will prove I'm responsible, and I will belong.**

Most of us strive to be responsible adults, whether that's taking care of our finances or being a good role model to our children. However, there are certain things that we simply cannot control in the world.

Some of us have a hard time knowing where to draw the line between "preparing for the worst" and "always anticipating the worst is going to happen." When we live in the space of the latter, where our responsibility extends to every outcome under the sun, we tend to get so wrapped up in our worries that we lose touch with the people and events going on around us.

As you ask yourself the following questions, try not to think too hard about your response. Trust your gut and answer yes or no.

1. How often do you find yourself running with a story before knowing all the facts?
2. Do you plan around "worst-case scenarios" in your job, in relationships, on trips—maybe with everything?
3. Do you find it hard to enjoy the moment? Are you constantly waiting for the other shoe to drop?
4. Do you struggle to give people the benefit of doubt?
5. Do you find it difficult to just relax without a problem to solve?
6. Do you often have a knot of anxiety in your gut and stressful thoughts running in your head?

While Tate tries to prevent bad things from happening, let's meet Callie and see how her unique False Belonging Habit impacts her life.

CHAPTER 6

CALLIE: REPRESSING EMOTIONS

Callie absentmindedly looked down at her manicured left hand. It still felt strange to see no band on her ring finger, even all these years after taking it off. Four years, in fact, almost to the day. With that realization, a swell of sadness built up within her, and soon she was fighting back tears.

Stop it, Callie, she scolded herself. *You're being ridiculous.*

She scanned the grocery store from her spot behind the counter in the floral department she managed. There were no customers around, so she decided to grab a coffee and collect herself.

As she headed to the dimly lit break room, she found her co-workers Rachel and Andrew. To Callie's surprise, Andrew was drinking from the mug with hot air balloons on it. "Why are you drinking from Zack's mug?" Callie asked, trying to distract herself from her burgeoning sadness.

"You didn't hear? He got sacked," Andrew responded flatly.

"What? Why?"

"I mean, do you really have to ask? He was always calling in sick, and if he did show up, he'd be in the bathroom for half of his shift…"

As Callie listened to Andrew gossip, she could feel a fire growing within her. "But he had a medical condition. A lot of that wasn't his fault," Callie defended.

"I mean, sure, you can play that card a few times. But c'mon, Callie, it'd gotten ridiculous," Andrew said, taking another sip from the mug.

The words were on the tip of her tongue. *Well, how about I remove half of your colon and see how you do, Andrew!*

She was so close to ripping into her callous colleague, but she locked her jaw. *Nothing good would come from speaking up*, she told herself. *You don't want to get a reputation for being difficult.* Instead, she poured coffee into her own designated cup: one with fluffy sheep in top hats that her son had picked out for her.

Rachel finished the last of her coffee and stood up to refill her mug. Suddenly, she let out a shriek. "Spider!"

Andrew hopped up, rolling up a newspaper on the table. Callie scanned the area until she saw it: a daddy long-legs.

"Wait!" Callie shrieked so loudly that Rachel jumped. "Sorry," Callie said. "But daddy long-legs are good! They eat a bunch of other bugs and even other spiders."

"Of course you'd know that," Andrew mumbled. "It's a spider. In the break room. I'm gonna kill it," he said, turning his attention back to the arachnid.

"Just, just let me catch it instead," Callie implored, frantically looking around for a cup. She snatched up a white Styrofoam one from the stack next to the coffee maker. She angled the cup just so, inched forward, and quickly secured the cup around the spider.

"Got it!" she announced.

As she lifted the cup away from the wall, trying to put the lid on, she pulled back a little too much. The daddy long-legs shot out as he desperately made his escape... straight towards Rachel.

"Ahhh!" Rachel screamed before quickly squashing the spider with her shoe. Callie's heart dropped.

Before she could stop them, tears welled in Callie's eyes.

"I'm so sorry, Callie. It was just instinct. It was coming toward me and I... I panicked," Rachel rattled off.

Callie stood with the cup still in her hand, frozen, staring at the crushed legs on the floor. Sadness swelled up inside her, and it took every ounce of effort to quash it back down.

"It's fine," Callie said, trying to hide her disappointment.

"Are you... upset about this? Seriously?" Andrew's voice was so sharp that it felt like a stab. Callie could feel the judgment radiating off him.

"I said it's fine," she repeated. She plastered a smile on her face. "It's just a spider. Anyway, I'm gonna get some air."

As soon as she'd walked out the door, Callie's smile fell and the tears returned. She shook her head. Why was she like this? It was just a spider!

Why couldn't she just be normal?

Callie's False Belonging Habit: I believe if I repress my emotions, I will belong.

Can you relate? How often do you try to hide or deny your feelings?

STRUGGLING TO FIT IN

The next day, Callie was in a much better mood. Today was a celebration! Her friend Melissa was getting married, and Callie was chock-full of excitement. As she stood in the hotel room, waiting for the bride to make her appearance, she smoothed down the front of her sleeveless, plum-colored dress.

"I tell ya, there's a reason women our age aren't bridesmaids," Callie's friend, Crystal, mumbled to her.

"What are you talking about? We look great!" Callie exclaimed, her gold bangles clanging together as she gestured enthusiastically. Callie got closer to the mirror, watching her reflection as she shook her arms over her head. "I mean, come on, the arm fat really adds to the look!" She jiggled her arms, laughing as Crystal giggled.

"Thank god you're here with me," Crystal said, giving Callie a side hug as the bride entered the suite.

"What do you all think?" Melissa asked the roomful of bridesmaids and family members.

A chorus of "Lovely!" and "Beautiful!" rang throughout the room.

"I've never seen a more gorgeous bride in my whole life!" Callie gushed. She ran forward and gave Melissa the biggest squeeze she could manage in her tight dress. "The hair! The makeup! Oh my gosh, are those pearls on your earrings?!" As Callie peppered the bride with questions, her eye caught Melissa's future mother-in-law and sister-in-law shooting Callie a look while whispering to each other.

"They are pearls! I thought they'd accent the dress nicely," Melissa said, touching the earrings delicately.

"They do! Everything is just perfect" Callie hugged Melissa once more.

"Okay, okay," Melissa's mother-in-law swooped in, shooting a condescending look at Callie. "How about we let the bride rest for a minute, huh?"

As Melissa was led away, Callie felt herself growing hot. She'd seen that look so many times before. She had done it again—been *too* excited. Made everyone uncomfortable. *Get it together and stay calm today*, Callie told herself. *Don't make yourself the center of attention. It's not your day!*

Before long, the bridal party made their way to the ceremony space, and Callie bawled her eyes out at the touching vows. At least this was an *acceptable* time to cry.

After photos were taken, everyone was led to the reception space. The bride and groom had split the wedding party among the tables, so Callie didn't know most of the people she was sitting with. At least she was reunited with her seven-year-old son, Liam, who had been watched by a friend as Callie fulfilled her bridesmaid duties.

"Mom, can I take this off? It's itchy," Liam said, pulling at his tie.

"Not quite yet," Callie said, rubbing his back.

As Callie started making small talk with the group, the MC announced that the first dance was about to begin. She watched with a loving smile as her friend of over a decade danced with her new husband. Liam swayed in the chair next to her, and Callie felt so genuinely overjoyed that Melissa had found the love of her life.

But as that thought played in Callie's mind, another darker thought swam in. *You'll never find love again. You're too much. No one wants to be with you.* An intense grief overcame Callie, intermixing with the happiness she felt for her friend.

The duality of emotions was overwhelming. How could she be so happy and heartbroken at once?

The tears came out of nowhere, without time to stop them, threatening the makeup she had just reapplied. Out of the corner of her eye, she noticed a couple, who were friends with the groom, seeming to hold back laughter. On the other side of them, an aunt of Melissa's pursed her lips in seeming disapproval.

Liam pulled on Callie's dress. "Mom, why are you the only one crying?"

Callie shook her head, unable to answer. She couldn't focus or think about anything else right now. All she could feel was this grief that threatened to overtake her.

Once the first dance ended, Callie could feel that sadness starting to fade. She took Liam's hand in hers. "Let's go to the bathroom."

"I don't have to..." Liam started, but Callie was already up and leading him across the room. She found a family bathroom and walked in, locking the door behind them. She covered her face with her hands as the memories of all the staring and disapproval hit her. She'd made a fool of herself, again, even though she promised herself she wouldn't. *Why can't I just control my emotions? Everyone else seems to be able to do it just fine!*

"Why are we in the bathroom?" Liam asked.

"Mom just needed a little time away from those people."

"Why?"

"Because I was being too much," Callie answered.

"Too much?" Liam asked with furrowed brows.

"You'll understand when you're older," Callie said.

"I'm sorry you feel bad," he said with a shrug. Callie bent down and hugged her son tightly.

One day, before too long, Liam was going to realize that his mother couldn't control her emotions. Would these outbursts scare him off, too? Just like they had his father?

A new wave of tears threatened to cascade down her face, but she willed them away.

I have to do better. For him.

GIVING EMOTIONS A CHANCE

After the wedding, Callie found herself in a deep funk. She wasn't her usual enthusiastic self at work, and her coworkers noticed. One afternoon, the colleague Callie was closest to, Yasmine, invited Callie to have lunch with her outside at the picnic table over their break.

"I haven't seen you like this before," Yasmine said, taking a bite out of her chicken wrap. "I'm worried about you."

Callie didn't even look up from her container of fried rice leftovers. "Well, maybe this is how I'm supposed to be. Quiet. Composed. At least nobody is looking at me for once."

"But it's not *you!*" Yasmine countered.

As they spoke, a man rode up on his bicycle. Yasmine and Callie both recognized him as one of their favorite regular customers.

"Hey you two!" Rowan said as he got off his bike. "I saw you back here and thought I'd stop by to say hi."

"Rowan! Beautiful day, isn't it?" Yasmine asked.

"Just the perfect temperature," Rowan said.

Callie gave Rowan a polite smile before returning her attention to her leftovers. "Yeah, it's nice."

Rowan furrowed his brow. "I think that's the shortest sentence I've ever heard from you, Callie. Is everything all right?"

Yasmine elbowed Callie. "See? This isn't you." Callie shrugged in response.

Yasmine turned to Rowan. "She thinks she's too emotional, so she's trying to be 'normal.'"

Callie shot Yasmine a look. She didn't want Yasmine telling everyone about her business.

"I consider myself pretty emotional," Rowan said. "Does that make me 'abnormal?'"

Callie quickly looked up, aghast. "Of course not!" Then she sighed. "You guys just don't understand how embarrassing I am."

Now the wound reopened. She remembered everyone's eyes on her at the wedding, the stifled laughter, the whispered judgements. Before she knew it, tears were streaming down her face.

"Oh god, here I go again," Callie muttered, rolling her eyes.

Rowan sat down across from them at the picnic table. "There's no need to fight it. We don't care if you cry, do we, Yasmine?"

Yasmine shook her head. "Not at all. Actually, when I see you let loose like this, I'm kind of... jealous."

"Why?" Callie asked, almost appalled, as she dabbed at the still-flowing tears.

"I've never been able to do that. If I even hinted at being upset as a kid, my parents would shut it down. And it just stuck with me. You talk about not feeling normal? I feel like a weirdo because I *can't* cry."

"Oh," Callie said in surprise.

"Yasmine's not alone," Rowan said. "So many people are numb these days. When I met you, Callie, it was like a breath of fresh air."

"I guess you two are the exception then," Callie deflected. "Thanks for trying to make me feel better, though."

"Even if we are the exception, why bother with what the majority thinks? Why should they get to dictate how you experience your life?" Rowan asked.

"Well..." Callie searched for the answer, but she couldn't find the right words.

"He's got a good point, Callie," Yasmine added.

"I stopped trying to fit into the crowd a long time ago. Let me tell you, it's quite freeing," Rowan said. He glanced down at his watch. "Well, I better take care of my shopping before it gets too late. I hope you start feeling more like yourself soon, Callie."

Callie smiled timidly in response.

"See?" Yasmine said to Callie once they were alone again.

Callie barely heard her; she had a thousand thoughts running through her mind at once. "I think I should get back to work," she said, standing up.

"You sure? You still have a few minutes left," Yasmine said.

"Yeah, I'm sure. Thank you, though."

"Sure thing. I'll come check on you in a bit, okay?"

Dazed, Callie nodded, then grabbed her container of barely touched food and headed inside.

ACCEPTING ONESELF, EMOTIONS AND ALL

The next morning, Callie was running some errands around town with Liam, who had been on his best behavior all morning as his mom had promised him a treat after the errands were done. As soon as they left their last stop, though, Liam piped up. "That's the last place?"

Callie chuckled to herself. "Yes, that's the last one. So now... home!"

Liam leaned forward against his seat belt. "Mom! You said..."

"I know, I know," she laughed heartily. "We'll go get a treat now."

Callie had just the place in mind: The Hearth.

They walked into the restaurant and were led to a booth. Callie asked the waitress if Rowan was in, and within a few moments Rowan bounded out of the kitchen door.

"Callie! And oh my, you must be Liam," Rowan said.

Liam sank down against the back of the booth, suddenly acting shy.

Callie laughed. "Say hello to Rowan, Liam."

Liam stuck up a hand quickly, then sank back down.

"Well, I'm so honored to have you two here! What can I do for you?"

"I brought Liam in for a treat!" Callie said, grinning at her son. He mirrored her smile.

"A treat, huh?" Rowan said. "What's your favorite dessert?"

"Ice cream," Liam whispered.

"Let's make it the best scoop ever then! Vanilla, lavender, pistachio, or chocolate?" Rowan asked.

"Chocolate," Liam said, a little more confidently this time.

Rowan disappeared and soon came back with a bowl and an extra large scoop of creamy goodness. Liam's eyes grew wide. He practically dove into the bowl with his spoon as the adults laughed.

As Liam ate, the adults caught up. "Any other big plans for the weekend?" Rowan asked.

"Well, I was hoping to go see some of the blooming wildflowers, but I'm not sure I'll get the chance," Callie said.

"Actually, some of my friends and I are gonna hike Beaver Tooth Trail tomorrow morning to check them out," Rowan said. "At some point, we'll find a good spot and just sit and talk about anything that's going on for us. It's a really open, safe space to talk about, feel, share... whatever. You're welcome to join us."

Callie considered this. "Liam is going to be spending the morning with my folks..."

"Helping Gramps with the baby cows!" Liam chimed in.

Callie laughed. "Yes, helping with the newborn calves. So sure! I'm in!"

After Rowan gave her the details, Callie sat back in her seat, more excited than she'd been in a while. Rowan had seen Callie in her full-blown emotional state, and yet he still wanted to spend time with her. If his friends were anything like him, this could be just what Callie needed.

Callie was the last to arrive at the trailhead the next morning. "I'm so glad you could make it!" Rowan greeted her before introducing her to everyone. Amani, Tate, and Kenta all welcomed her as the group started walking down the trail. The sun was just peeking through the holes in the tree coverage, and there was a coolness in the shadows. Callie breathed in the morning air; she couldn't remember the last time she'd been on a hike without her son. She enjoyed sharing her knowledge with the group, pointing out different flowers and plants.

After a couple miles, there was a clearing on the side of the trail situated perfectly under a huge oak tree. "This looks like a great place for a break," Rowan announced.

Everyone took out their water bottles and sat in a circle on the grass as a symphony of chirps and insect clicks played in the background.

"Callie, remember how I said we took some time during our hike to talk about how we're all doing? Well, there's a specific format we use," Rowan said. "Amani, care to explain?" he asked, taking a swig from his water bottle.

"So, we each get five minutes to check in," Amani explained. "It can be about anything we want—happy, sad, whatever. It's just a space to be completely open. Then, after the five minutes, we move to the next person."

"Sounds great!" Callie said.

"Also, we don't respond to each person's check in," Amani continued. "This is just a space to be vulnerable, with no risk of being judged or trying to fix or solve anything. It's just about putting it out there and letting it be received."

"Oh," Callie said. "Huh. Interesting idea."

"I can start," Tate offered. Kenta started his phone's timer. "So I've had a pretty good week overall. Since school got out, the girls have been spending the afternoons with me at the office. And I have this weird struggle going on. Like on the one hand, I *love* having them there with me and getting to show them the produce and what we do. But on the other hand, I feel like my productivity has shot down. Then I feel guilty because I know so many parents would love to have the opportunity to take their kids to work with them."

As Tate shared, the others listened intently, nodding but remaining silent. Once the timer went off, Callie almost responded to Tate's story, but caught herself.

Amani was next in the circle. "You know, I'm just feeling so proud of myself! I feel like I've really upped my game at work the past few weeks. My boss even pulled me into her office the other day to ask if I'd want to present at another conference..."

After her five minutes were up, Kenta was next.

"Actually, the past few days have been pretty awful. That woman I've been seeing, Angela, said she wanted to end things out of the blue. When I asked her why, she said I just 'wasn't what she needed in a man right now.' What does that even mean? I keep replaying that damn sentence in my head over and over. It's been haunting me! I can just tell what a hit my confidence has taken, and I'm trying not to take it personally. But, man, this has cut deep. So, yeah, I'm not doing great."

There was a pause for nearly a minute as Kenta took a few slow, deep breaths, then nodded.

"You still have a few minutes, Kenta. Anything else you want to say?" Rowan asked.

"No, I'm good."

Now, it was Callie's turn. Oddly, she felt a nervousness rise in her gut. What should she talk about? "Um, it's been a pretty good week. Liam had a swim meet and tumbling practice. I was in a wedding last weekend..." Callie thought about just glossing over the negatives of the event, but she remembered how open everyone else was. Why didn't she give it a shot, too?

"Actually, it was going great, and then I screwed it all up. I was watching the first dance, and I got all worked up about being alone, like I always do. It was stupid," she huffed, shaking her head.

108

"You don't have to discount your feelings here, Callie," Amani said quietly.

Callie looked around at the others, expecting someone to disagree with Amani's sentiment. But they each sat with gentle, encouraging smiles on their faces.

"Oh… um, thank you," Callie said. Sitting here, with this group of people, she had that same feeling of safety that she'd experienced with Rowan at the picnic table. This time, she decided to lean into it. "I went through a pretty bad divorce. My ex said some awful things to me, and to our friends about me. He even made up these accusations that I had bipolar disorder because I'm so… emotional. I've always seemed to have bigger feelings than everyone else, but the way he weaponized that part of me… it was brutal." Callie's voice started cracking.

"Ever since, I've seen the looks people give me and… it got to me. It still gets to me. I've been trying to keep my emotions in check, but that only seems to make it worse."

As the tears touched Callie's cheeks, the timer went off. Kenta reached out to gently touch her shoulder, and when she looked at him, she could see he had some misty eyes himself.

"You can keep going if you need to, Callie," Tate said.

"No, no, my time's up," she sniffled, wiping her nose with her sleeve.

"Really, we'd love to hear more," Amani said.

Everyone's nodding heads gave Callie the confidence to continue—to talk more about her fear of loneliness, as well as not being the mother she wanted to be for Liam. The few tears slowly turned into more, eventually transforming into heavy sobs.

"I'm sorry," she said at one point, barely able to get the words out.

"There's no need to apologize, Callie," Rowan replied kindly.

As Callie spoke, she could feel that heaviness in her gut begin to lighten. The worry seemed lessened, and the tears slowed. The sadness had just needed to run its course.

When her eyes were finally dry, Callie took a huge breath, letting it totally fill her lungs. Her whole being felt calmer. "Thank you, all of you. Being able to get that out meant a lot to me."

"Glad we could be here for you," Rowan said. "Do you have anything else to add?"

Callie shook her head. Kenta restarted the timer as Rowan spoke.

"This week has been hard for me. I had lunch with my mom the other day. She hasn't been feeling well lately. She hasn't had the energy to get out of bed, which isn't like her at all. She has a doctor's appointment next week where we'll hopefully find some answers, but..." Rowan's voice cracked. He closed his eyes and breathed in slowly.

When Rowan's eyes reopened, they were glossy with tears. "If something's wrong with her, I just don't know what I'm going to do. I've always had her to turn to. She's been my rock. I can't imagine what I'd do without her." As he talked, the tears flowed.

"As I've been worrying about this, I keep having flashbacks of things Mom has done throughout my life, just remarkable things. But she never made a big deal about any of it." Rowan swallowed hard, wiping away a tear from his chin.

As he talked about his mom, his tears continued to flow. He had to pause many times to collect himself, unable to speak. Callie watched him intently. This man, who always knew the right thing to say, who seemed to have everything figured out, was unabashedly letting his emotions show. He wasn't trying to hide his tears, wasn't ashamed of what he was feeling. He was allowing himself to be human.

Looking around the group, Callie recognized that no one was put off by his emotions, either. Amani was crying right along with Rowan, giving him a look that said she understood his pain, while Kenta and Tate offered quiet support. No one was rolling their eyes or shaking their heads at him.

Witnessing this, Callie felt the walls she had built start to come down. Maybe she didn't have to hide her emotions to fit in with the rest of the world.

Maybe she could let herself be human, too.

A MOMENT IN THE MIRROR: REPRESSING EMOTIONS

Within yourself, can you recognize Callie's False Belonging Habit: **I believe if I repress my emotions, I will belong.**

Most of us can objectively agree that emotions are a healthy part of life. As we'll learn in Part 2, our emotions are the direct highway to our innermost truths. Our feelings are what allow us to truly connect with our sense of belonging.

Yet there are those of us, like Callie, who go down a shame spiral after we show our feelings to the world. We worry about what others think of our display, wondering if we made a fool of ourselves. We condemn our feelings as being "inappropriate" or "too much." And as a result, we push our emotions down, hiding them away so we can be seen as "normal."

To determine if this False Belonging Habit applies to you, use these questions to explore your relationship with your emotions.

1. Do you fear your emotions?
2. Do you tell yourself your emotions don't matter?
3. Do you tend to isolate when you are feeling emotional?
4. Do you bury your feelings so deeply that you can feel sick with anxiety?
5. Do you overexplain or apologize for your emotions?
6. Do you replay the times you expressed your emotions, feeling ashamed just thinking about those moments?

It's now time to discover our last False Belonging Habit. Let's see how Nolan's Habit is holding him back.

CHAPTER 7

NOLAN: OVERWHELMED BY SELF-DOUBT

Nolan stared at the steak sitting on his plate. He had ordered medium, and this was definitely a very red medium rare. His grip tightened on his fork and knife as he tried to figure out what to do. He'd heard that rare beef can make you sick; at the same time, cooking shows seemed to talk up how rarer steak had a more robust tasting experience.

"Noli?" his mother asked. From her tone, it was clear this wasn't the first time she'd said his name.

"Yeah?"

"Everything okay with your steak?"

"Um, it's okay to eat this, right?" Nolan asked, pointing to the steak.

"Oh, it's fine," his dad said dismissively before cutting into his rare steak.

Nolan nodded, then cut a small piece from the outer edge.

"So, Tori, how is work going for you?" Nolan's mother asked.

"It's going great! Really great, actually." Tori looked over to Nolan, taking an expectant breath. "Actually, the company has asked me if I'd be open to relocating."

"Oh?" Nolan's father said. Nolan noted the new upswing in his tone.

"Yeah!" Tori replied. "They actually said they need someone in their Paris office, which would be just amazing!"

Nolan smiled and nodded along as Tori spoke, his internal monologue running wild. Nolan had always wanted to go to Paris—to actually live there would be next level! He'd been so excited when Tori shared the news, and he felt that same excitement bubbling up within him now.

After a brief pause, Nolan's mom asked, "So, you two would do... long distance?"

Now Nolan looked over at his mother, who was giving him one of those wide-eyed looks she'd get when she was highly skeptical about something.

"Well..." Tori looked again to Nolan for support, but he was still locking eyes with his mom. "We'd actually talked about Nolan going with me."

"You're thinking of moving to *France*, Noli?" his mom asked. Nolan could tell she was trying to keep her tone light, but he knew she was hiding her true feelings.

Doubt crept in. Was he being foolish? Rash? Maybe this was a terrible idea, and he and Tori had just gotten swept up in the moment.

"It's not a sure thing. They haven't even offered Tori the job yet," Nolan said.

"I mean, they basically have. They're just putting the paperwork together for me to sign," Tori corrected. "Nolan, I told you, it's mine if I want it." She was enunciating more than usual. His parents probably didn't even notice, but Nolan knew she was annoyed. Very annoyed.

"Oh, yeah. I mean, it would be a great opportunity," Nolan said, nodding as he looked into Tori's twinkling hazel eyes. Man, was Nolan head over heels for Tori. And getting to experience the most romantic city in the world together? He couldn't imagine anything better. He smiled at the thought.

But then his father asked, "What about your job, Nolan? What would you do for work?"

Nolan stared not so much *at* his dad as *through* him as he considered his new dilemma. What *would* he do for work? Of course the question had gone through his mind, but he'd been so focused on Tori that he'd pushed it away. Would he be able to find work? What if he couldn't? How would they afford living in France's capital?

"We haven't gotten that far yet," Nolan said, careful to not give too direct of an answer.

"Well, it would certainly be a learning opportunity, wouldn't it?" his mom asked. That tone. Was she being sincere, or was that sarcasm?

Nolan unconsciously smoothed down the polo shirt his parents had given him for his birthday. It *would* be quite the learning experience—but what if it was one of those you-learn-from-your-biggest-mistakes kind of experiences?

Nolan stared off into the distance, his mind running through a hundred different scenarios at once. What if he hates the food? What if the French people are mean? Was he going to have to learn French? How long would that take him? What if Tori didn't like her new position? What happens if he gets sick? Would he have to get a different phone plan?

Underlying every thought was one fundamental fact in Nolan's mind: he had to make sure he made the *right* decision.

"Well…" Nolan said, sensing he had missed some of the conversation and it was his turn to speak, "it's just an idea right now. No need to put too much weight into it yet."

He glanced over at Tori, who wasn't hiding her grimace. That wasn't good. She was upset. Putting down his fork, Nolan decided to change topics. "How is everyone's food?"

"Good," his father said, taking a sip of his cocktail.

"Mine's good," Tori murmured, moving her green beans around on her plate.

"Delicious," his mother said, looking down at her roast chicken. "You?"

Nolan didn't want to complain about how his steak was cooked. And the more he ate, the more he realized it wasn't bad. Maybe he did like it?

"It's… interesting," Nolan finally said.

Tori huffed beside him, shaking her head. "That's Nolan's favorite way to describe anything."

What did she mean by that? Nolan tried to analyze that comment, but his father changed the topic to the local football team's losing streak. Figuring he'd smooth things over with her later, he turned his attention to his dad, taking another bite of that okay-but-not-okay steak.

Nolan's False Belonging Habit: I believe if I make the "right" decision, regardless of what I actually think, I will belong.

Can you relate? Do you second-guess yourself and have a hard time making a decision?

DENYING SELF-DOUBT

"I can't believe you didn't back me up!" Tori huffed after Nolan's parents had dropped them off at his apartment.

"I... I'm just not sure what I think about all of it yet," Nolan said, closing the front door behind him.

"*You* were excited about it! You said so!"

Nolan remembered what he'd said. But was he really excited? Or had he just been so caught up in Tori's enthusiasm that he agreed? He tended to do that.

"Yeah, I guess I did."

"*Are* you excited?"

Nolan hated this kind of direct question. He didn't know what to believe. There were so many pros and cons! He couldn't decide just like that.

"I don't know, maybe?"

"This isn't a 'maybe' question, Nolan! Trust your gut for once. Are you excited or not?"

"I mean, yeah." Just as quickly as he'd agreed, Nolan felt that uncertainty rise back up. His parents had had a good point. What was he going to do for work? Was he throwing his career away? He'd never lived that far away from his folks, either. How would he cope with that? What if they needed something and he was half a world away?

"Nolan!" Tori yelled.

Nolan jumped. He must have been in his head too long again. "There's just so much to consider."

"Ahhh!" Tori screamed, throwing her hands in the air. "Every time! You do this *every* time I ask you to make a decision. Where do you want to go for dinner? 'Where do you want to go?' What movie do you want to see? 'I've heard good things about this one, but this one has this actor...' but then you don't give an answer! I don't care that there's a lot to consider. I just want you to think for yourself for once and make a damn choice!"

Nolan's heart raced as he watched his girlfriend pace around the room. They'd had arguments about his indecisiveness before, but nothing like this.

"If you can't make a decision about something this important to me, I just don't see how we can keep doing this," Tori said.

"I just need some more time to think about it," Nolan said.

Tears started forming in Tori's eyes. "No, you don't. I've dealt with this for two years, Nolan. I can't anymore."

Nolan felt like the air had been sucked out of his lungs. "What are you talking about?"

"I love you so much. So much. But I can't live in this constant state of indecisiveness. It's exhausting! I want a partner—" She stopped herself. "I *deserve* a partner who isn't afraid to give their opinion, even if it's different from mine. Who isn't paralyzed whenever they're asked to make a decision."

"I'm not *paralyzed*..." Nolan started.

"Oh really? What about that talk we had, what, two months ago? When my friends invited us to go to that Vegas show with them. I asked you and you hemmed and hawed about it so long that they sold out of tickets."

"Well, that was a special situation," Nolan countered.

"Why?" She asked, her voice catching.

"That was during tax season. You know how crazy my office gets that time of year. I couldn't even think about anything else."

"Right, right. That same old excuse!" Tori huffed through the tears that were now running down her cheeks. "And it's not just that. When we talk about marriage, you go back and forth between it being 'an antiquated system' and 'a great testament to love.' When I asked if you'd be open to raising your kids Jewish, you said you'd have to do a lot of research into it first. I want to get married one day. I want to have kids. And right now, I want to move to Paris! And if I stay with you, I just don't know if any of that is going to happen."

Now Nolan was really getting scared. Where was all this coming from? He felt like he was a great boyfriend. Sure, there were little things Tori helped him with. She usually picked out his outfits for big events, and she often suggested their weekend plans. But he could always make her laugh when she was down, and he would drop everything to help whenever she needed him.

Most importantly, he loved her more than anything else.

Nolan had to figure out what to say—the perfect thing—to convince Tori he could make a decision. But for once, instead of running through a million different scenarios, his mind was empty. He couldn't think of a single way to prove he could be the person she wanted him to be.

"Yeah, I figured you wouldn't have a response for that," she said, crossing her arms.

Nolan's eyes started to burn. "Tori, we'll figure this out. We just have to talk about it more."

She shook her head. "I'm done talking."

Before Nolan could say anything else, Tori turned and walked out the door.

Nolan stared at the doorknob, debating whether he should go after her. Did she want some time alone? Would chasing after her only make it worse? Or did she want to see him fight for her?

As he stood contemplating his options, he heard a car start and drive away.

He'd missed his chance.

THE HEAVY WEIGHT OF SELF-DOUBT

Nolan's hand shook as he stared at the photo on his phone. It was a post from Tori's social media—her flight itinerary to Paris.

This was real. She was leaving. Without him.

Nolan's legs suddenly turned to Jell-O, and he collapsed onto his couch. This couldn't be happening. Sure, she hadn't returned his calls or texts. Even the flowers he had sent were marked as "undeliverable." But he figured this was all temporary, that they'd still end up together.

It was clear now, though. He had lost her.

The stomach cramps came first. He could feel his intestines knotting themselves up tighter and tighter as he rocked back and forth, his mind racing. Why hadn't he just agreed to go to France? He would have learned to like it. It would have been a new, amazing experience. Or why didn't he run after her that day she left his apartment? Why didn't he fight for her, tell her that she was everything to him?

Why couldn't he make a damn decision to save his life?

He threw the phone on the adjoining cushion and fully bent over, wrapping his arms under his thighs. Now the panic moved upward to his chest and his heart started racing like he'd just run a marathon.

Tori was right. How was he ever going to achieve anything if he couldn't make a simple decision? How was he ever going to have a successful relationship if he crumbled every time he tried to discuss marriage or kids?

He was going to be alone for the rest of his miserably indecisive life.

Nolan closed his eyes tight, shaking his head. The nausea finally worked its way up his throat. Every inch of his body felt ill, felt in pain.

Nolan just knew that there was no getting rid of the feeling. *I'm stuck with it, forever. There's no escaping who I am.*

It had been days since Nolan saw Tori's social media post, and he'd been fundamentally broken ever since. He'd called in sick to work and barely had the motivation to get out of bed every day.

The self-doubt had gotten so bad that he found himself slipping into a darkness that he'd never before experienced. Every negative thought that he'd ever had about himself seemed to be stuck on repeat. How he'd ruined everything with Tori. How he'd never add up to anything if he couldn't make a decision. How his professional career was destined for failure. How his friends probably couldn't stand him either... Each judgmental thought snowballed on the one before until Nolan was so depressed that he could barely function.

Then, Nolan had a thought. He made the strenuous trek to the bathroom and pulled out a bottle of oxycodone that he'd gotten after his knee surgery last spring. He'd only taken a couple then, but he remembered how much they numbed the pain. How much they numbed *everything.* And right now, all Nolan wanted was to be numb from these barraging thoughts. So, he threw some pills in his mouth and swallowed.

The knock on his front door echoed in Nolan's bathroom. Maybe if he ignored whoever it was, they'd just go away.

"Noli!" his mother's muffled voice yelled.

Nolan sighed. He knew his mother would wait until he answered. So, he slowly shuffled over to the door.

"Hey," he mumbled, opening the door just enough for his mother to see his face.

"I just saw Tori's post. She got a flight to Paris?" his mother asked.

Nolan felt his stomach tighten.

"Here, open the door more, I can barely see you," his mom said, pushing the door open.

Nolan relented, embarrassed that his mother could see the full scale of Nolan's situation. The sink was overflowing with dirty dishes. The counter was a mess of stains and splatters. Empty energy drink cans and takeout boxes covered his coffee table. Then there was Nolan himself; he hadn't showered in days, and his normally neatly coiffed black hair was oily enough to wax the floor.

Nolan couldn't bring himself to make eye contact with his mother. Should he tell her about the breakup? Or was it better if he didn't bring it up?

As Nolan mentally prepared for how to explain himself, his mother opened her mouth. "Did you decide to stay here then? And you'll still work with the accounting firm? Then would you do long distance? I've known people that it's worked for, but it can be really hard, too. But it depends how long she's out there. Does she know? Is it like a six-month thing? Or are you still thinking of joining her at some point? Once she's more established there, that might make it easier on you…"

Nolan felt himself slouching down further and further, feeling as if each new question added more weight to his shoulders.

"Ma," Nolan cut in, "I just can't do this right now."

His mother scrunched her eyebrows at him. "What? Are you coming down with something?"

"Sure," Nolan managed to get out.

"You should go lie down. Drink some tea. But not if it's your stomach, that might upset it more, you know."

Nolan nodded. "Will do."

"I'll let you rest then. But think about what I said. This is a huge decision you're making."

Nolan nodded again. He mumbled goodbye and slowly closed the door. He took a deep breath, relishing the much-needed silence.

His mother was exhausting. And frustrating. She didn't even ask how he was, even though he looked terrible, because she was so focused on talking through every possible scenario...

And that's when it clicked. *This* is what Tori had been talking about when it came to Nolan's indecisiveness. How had Nolan never seen it before? That he was just like his mother? That he was equally as exhausting, frustrating, and even... somewhat heartless?

All that weight on Nolan's shoulders seemed to double. Shoulders slumped, he shuffled over to his couch and sat, covering his face with his palms.

He started thinking over his childhood, and how nervous his mother was about every decision. If they went to an amusement park, she'd bring up that they should have gone to a water park. She was just never satisfied with the choice she'd made, and it brought everyone else down a little.

And now Nolan wondered: how long had he been robbing himself of joy by living this way? What else could he have accomplished—experienced—if he didn't have this doubt controlling his brain?

He thought about that Vegas trip he and Tori didn't go on because he couldn't decide on if he'd like the band. Their friends had come back and said it was the best concert they'd ever been to. That it was one of the most fun trips they'd been on in years.

He thought back to his college graduation and choosing his career path. He had lost ten pounds before getting his diploma, physically sick from deciding what to do next with his life. After much deliberation and discussion with his parents, he had settled on the safest option.

Then there was Tori. She was so full of adventure and life, and he just couldn't keep up with her.

As these memories swarmed his mind, the impending realization became clearer and clearer. He had inherited his doubt from his mother, and he had been like this for 25 years.

Nolan felt trapped. He'd already felt like he'd hit rock bottom, but apparently he still had farther to fall. The hopelessness encompassed every molecule of his being. Desperate to stop this feeling from overtaking him, he moved to the bathroom, emptied the remaining few pills into his hand, and quickly took them.

He plopped down to watch TV. As he started feeling the calming effects of the medication, he flipped to a basketball game.

He eyed his basketball shoes near his bedroom door. He hadn't played in a while. Maybe some exercise would do him good.

The more the pills took over his brain, the more he thought that shooting some hoops sounded like a great idea. So, he changed, grabbed his basketball, and headed to the park.

COLLAPSING UNDER DOUBT

When Nolan arrived at the park, he saw a middle-aged man standing by himself on the basketball court, checking his watch.

Nolan decided to stretch a bit before shooting some hoops. The pills were starting to kick in, and he felt so... relaxed. He sat down on the grass and watched as a couple cars pulled up. Two men and three women got out, along with a young boy.

"Tate!" one of the women yelled.

"I wasn't expecting a whole cheering squad for helping Mia practice," the man on the court said with a laugh.

"Oh, we're here to play," one of the men said, bending down into a competitive stance.

Nolan watched as they all said their hellos, and a little boy ran around and gave each of them hugs.

The boy was the first to spot Nolan. He gave him a quick wave, and Nolan waved back.

Nolan listened as one of them explained how to play the game "Horse." Nolan couldn't help chuckling to himself; who didn't know how to play "Horse"?

The younger woman glanced over at him, and Nolan stopped laughing. Did she hear him? Should he apologize? Or would that make it more of a thing? He didn't mean anything by it...

"Basically, we take turns shooting. One of us takes a shot, and then the rest of us have to stand in the same spot and try to make the same shot. If we miss, we add a letter. If you end up spelling out horse, you're out," one of the guys explained.

"Get ready to go down, Mia! I'm gonna send you to the glue factory!" another yelled.

Nolan couldn't help but laugh, more loudly than he realized. The group now all looked over at him.

"Oh, um, sorry," Nolan said, still chuckling.

"Do you play?" one of the men asked Nolan.

"Yeah," Nolan said.

"Want to join?"

"Uh…" Normally, Nolan would be running through all the scenarios of joining: were they just being polite? Would he actually be crashing their game? But with the chemical confidence running through his veins, he made up his mind more quickly than usual. "Sure, that'd be great."

"Fantastic, well, I'm Rowan," the man said. "And this is Tate, Kenta, Amani, Mia, Callie, and Callie's son, Liam. And you are?"

"Nolan," Nolan said. "Nice to meet you, and thanks for the offer. It's been a while since I've played with anyone."

"Happy to have you," Amani said. "And, please, go easy on us. We're not that good."

"Speak for yourself!" Mia called, grabbing the ball and sinking a clean two-pointer.

"Yay!" everyone cheered.

"*Avive la vie!*" Mia hollered with a big grin.

Nolan looked at her curiously.

"Live life to the fullest," Mia explained. "It's a Rowan phrase."

"Huh," Nolan said, eyeing Rowan curiously.

Amani waved off her turn and let Kenta go first.

"Like this?" Kenta shot, and the ball fell about a foot short of the basket. Kenta's cheeks reddened, and his shoulders sank slightly.

Then, from the other side of the court, Amani started hooting and hollering. "Hey, when you're on our level, you have to celebrate every shot—hit or miss!" Callie joined in and cheered from her chair, grabbing Liam's hand and raising their arms up high.

Kenta smiled, clearly appreciating their silly support.

"Rowan, you're up… where's Rowan?" Tate asked.

Nolan started looking around, only to find Rowan nowhere on the court.

"There he is," Mia announced, pointing across the street.

There was an older woman standing next to a car with its trunk open, and Rowan was grabbing grocery bags and carrying them inside her house.

"Well, I guess I'll get my cardio in," Mia said under her breath. She ran across the court and street to help.

Nolan looked around at the remaining faces. His indecisiveness managed to creep back in. Should he help too? Or would that be weird for him to go?

"Should I go too?" Nolan finally asked, hoping Tate may make the decision for him.

"Up to you," Tate said. "I'm gonna stay right here," he added, dribbling the ball.

Nolan's eyes darted between Kenta and Amani chatting at the far end of the court, Tate staring intently at his dribbling, Callie and Liam talking in their chairs, and Rowan and Mia carrying bags inside. It was awkward for Nolan to just stand here. He should probably go join someone's conversation. But whose? Would it be weird to go up to Callie and her son? Amani and Kenta seemed deep in conversation about something.

"Thanks for helping," Mia said, jogging past Nolan on her way over to Tate.

Nolan cursed himself silently. *I should've gone and helped.*

With everyone finally back on the court, Tate tossed Rowan the ball.

"All right, here we go," Rowan said, closing his eyes. He stood for a few seconds, breathing.

"Rowan, this isn't meditation," Mia jabbed. "Just shoot!"

Rowan didn't seem bothered by Mia. After taking another breath, he opened his eyes, shot, and missed.

Before anyone could grab the ball, Mia snatched it up. "Okay, I know you have been having fun and all, but I need to actually practice for my league. That's why I asked Tate to come. What if we switch it up and play three on three?"

Now the group got into a real game. Nolan was feeling even looser, and that was reflected in his game.

"Here, here!" Tate yelled at Kenta, who was cornered behind Rowan. As Kenta threw the ball, Nolan jumped over, grabbed the ball, and shot in one fluid motion. It swooshed in the basket.

"Damn it!" Tate muttered. Nolan watched Tate wipe sweat off his forehead. He was good. Nolan figured he must have played in school, maybe even college.

After another twenty minutes of hard play up and down the court, Rowan asked, "Can we take a water break?"

Nolan looked over to see Rowan, Kenta, and Amani all quite winded. Tate was also breathing pretty hard, but he didn't seem to want to admit it.

"Good idea. Do you want to keep playing while they rest? You two against me?" Tate asked Nolan and Mia.

Mia nodded her head furiously while Nolan wiped his forehead with his shirt. He was drenched in sweat and feeling pretty tired himself. Did he want to stop? Or would he look weak if he did?

"I'll play for a bit longer," Nolan said, striking a compromise in his head.

As Tate shot the ball, they entered a new level of competition. Amani, Rowan, Kenta, Callie, and Liam watched as the three battled it out on the court. Mia tried to elbow her way in, but she couldn't hang with the experience of the other two.

Nolan's face felt very flushed, almost alarmingly so. He was sweating much more now too. Why was he sweating so much? Then, after making a quick jump to his left, he had to stand still for a second to get his bearings. He was dizzy all of a sudden.

"You feeling okay, Nolan?" Rowan called from the sidelines.

Nolan ignored him, locked into the game.

Soon Mia needed to step aside to catch her breath, but Nolan and Tate kept going. They shot, then rebounded, then ran, then shot. The ball bounced off the backboard, and Tate and Nolan both jumped for it. But midair, the sun seemed to become extra blinding. Black spots started blocking Nolan's vision, and everything became very blurry. He was so lightheaded...

In a split second, Nolan lost all spatial awareness. As he came back down to Earth, his legs didn't catch him like they should have. Instead, he fell into Tate's trajectory—who landed directly on Nolan's left leg. As he did, Nolan's ankle bent at an unnatural angle.

"Are you okay?" Tate asked.

Nolan couldn't respond. His eyes were so heavy—maybe he'd just take a quick rest.

"Nolan? Nolan!" Tate said.

The Crew jumped into action. Mia called 911 as Rowan knelt down beside Nolan. He was breathing, but barely. His pulse was racing.

They propped his head up with their jackets, dabbing his forehead with Callie's scarf as they waited for the ambulance to arrive.

"You're gonna be okay," Rowan said calmly. "You're okay."

AN ACT OF TRUE CONNECTION

The Crew arrived at the hospital as quickly as they could. Rowan and Mia arrived first, not long after the ambulance. As they approached the front desk, they overheard a few words from the EMTs who brought Nolan in: "Faint heartbeat." "Unresponsive." "Overdose." Unable to get any other information, they sat in the waiting room and waited for the others to arrive.

"You think he had a heart condition or something?" Amani asked as the rest of the group walked in.

"I don't know. Maybe," Callie answered, holding Liam's hand.

"What if he didn't even know he had it?" Kenta suggested.

"He's just so young…" Tate said.

"Poor guy," Amani whispered.

Finally, they spotted Rowan and Mia.

"How is he?" Tate asked.

Rowan sighed, rubbing his temples. "I'm not sure. We heard them say something about an overdose."

A silence settled over the group as they processed this information.

"What about his leg? It looked like I did some pretty good damage to it…" Tate said, his collar still sweaty from the game.

"That wasn't your fault," Amani quickly pointed out.

Tate shook his head in response, pacing around the room.

"Were they able to contact his family?" Callie asked.

Rowan shrugged. "I don't know."

They all sat quietly, contemplating what to do next.

Rowan was the first to speak up. "Well, I'm going to hunker down here for a while. Anyone care to join?"

"I'm not going anywhere until I get some answers," Tate said. "I won't be able to calm down until I do."

Mia crossed her arms. "Blaming yourself is just going to make your anxiety worse, dude. I mean, I'm the one who got us all together to play. I could be blaming myself too. But I'm not, because it was an accident."

"Mia's right," Kenta agreed. While Tate shrugged, his stomach let out a rumble. "How about I run over to that Thai restaurant across the way and grab some food?" Kenta offered.

"I gotta run home for lunch with the kids, but I can come back after for an hour or two," Amani said.

"Liam and I can hang out for a bit, too," Callie said.

Despite them just meeting Nolan, everyone could sense how important it was to be here—not only to make sure Nolan was okay, but also to support Tate through his feelings of guilt.

The next morning, Rowan and Tate could feel the effects of sleeping in the uncomfortable waiting room chairs overnight. The rest of the Crew had gone home, but Tate was so racked with guilt that he wouldn't leave until he found out if Nolan was okay. Rowan elected to wait with Tate to give him some company.

As Tate was stretching his neck, he spotted a familiar face walking in. "Whitney!" he said, jumping up.

The nurse looked over, clearly surprised to see him. "Tate? What are you doing here? Are the girls okay? Molly?"

"Oh yeah, they're fine. Great, actually. Nadia keeps asking when she can go back to your place to play with Tamara," Tate said with a tired smile.

"She's welcome anytime," Whitney said, relaxing a bit. "So why are you here?"

"It's a long story," Tate said, shaking his head. Then he perked up. "Actually, maybe you could help. We saw this guy get pretty hurt, and we—that's my friend, Rowan. Rowan, this is Whitney."

"Hello," Rowan said with a wave as Whitney responded with a nod.

"Anyway," Tate continued, "we just really want to make sure he's okay before we head home. His name's Nolan. We don't need any details or anything like that, but is there any chance you could just let us know how he is?"

Whitney considered this, then said, "Let me see what I can do."

Fifteen minutes later, she came back out to the waiting room. "He's going to be okay. Now go home. You look awful," she said, smiling at the end.

Tate and Rowan let out a collective sigh of relief and then took her advice.

FACING INSECURITIES

After a few days in the hospital, Nolan was doing much better. However, he had broken his ankle so badly that he needed to have surgery. This, coupled with his accidental overdose, meant he needed to stay in the hospital a bit longer for monitoring.

Nolan was watching a movie on the small mounted TV when his phone buzzed. It was a text from his mom. Are you over that stomach bug? Wanna catch a movie tonight with me and Dad?

Nolan leaned back further into his pillow. He had avoided telling his parents what had happened, so he didn't know how to respond. He'd text them back later and figure it out then.

As he put his phone down, a nurse came in. "You have a visitor, Nolan. Are you feeling up to seeing them?"

Nolan's eyebrows scrunched. Who would be here to see him?

"Uh, sure."

"Hey, Nolan," Rowan said as he entered the room, carrying a vase with some daisies in it. "Thought this could brighten up the place."

"Oh, thanks," Nolan said, surprised that this near-stranger had come to visit. Why was he here? Did Nolan say something to Rowan that he didn't remember?

"We were all worried about you, after everything that happened. So, I wanted to check in to see how you're doing."

"Okay, I guess," Nolan said, pulling his blanket up further.

Rowan looked around the room, spotting the movie. "Had many visitors?"

Nolan shrugged. "You're actually the first."

"Oh," Rowan said, nodding.

Suddenly, Nolan grew self-conscious. "My parents would have come, but... I didn't tell them I'm here." Nolan instantly regretted his statement. Why would he say that he didn't tell his own parents he was hurt? "To be clear, I didn't tell them because I don't want them to worry," Nolan said before Rowan had a chance to respond.

Rowan waited, making sure Nolan was done speaking. "Well, I'm just glad you're feeling better."

"I mean, I'll tell them eventually," Nolan continued. "They just don't need to know the details of how I broke it, you know?" Rowan didn't immediately respond. Nolan wondered if he was judging him. "I just haven't decided yet," Nolan added.

"Sounds like a lot is on your mind," Rowan said.

"It's just, I don't want to disappoint them. It's not like I have a drug problem or something. I *don't*. But what if they think I do? And then they won't trust me anymore. Though they've never had a problem trusting me... Maybe I'm overthinking it," Nolan went on, his internal dialogue finally working itself outward.

"You seem to have a lot of things you're still deciding on," Rowan said.

Nolan glanced up, remembering that he barely knew the person he was talking to. "Sorry for rambling on like that. But yeah. I guess I do."

Rowan pulled an uncomfortable-looking tan chair closer to Nolan's bed. "Well, if you had to choose, right now, to either tell them or not, what would you do?" he asked, sitting down.

"I... I don't know."

"If your mom called you right now and asked what you were up to, what would you say?"

"Well, with my luck she'd hear the beeps of the machine or something in the background and figure out I'm in a hospital. Then she'd go crazy with all these questions. Why am I here? What happened? Then do I tell her I'm admitted? Or I could tell her I'm just at the doctor? That'd probably be less of a headache. But she's gonna figure it out eventually. Then she'd call my dad over, and he'd ask the same questions. Then one of them would ask if Tori was here, and do I want to go into *that* over the phone? Or is it better to do that in person? It's gonna be a hard conversation, I don't know what the right time is..."

Rowan put his hands up. "Whoa, whoa, whoa. This sounds very stressful."

"I know! They're just so..."

"No, I mean hearing you think through all this. I'm overwhelmed just listening," Rowan said.

"Really?" Nolan asked.

"Yeah! Sure, there are a lot of things to consider, but what do *you* want to tell them? How do *you* feel about it?"

"I don't know," Nolan said, shaking his head.

"No wonder you're having a hard time making a decision. How can you decide something when you don't know how you feel about it?"

Nolan didn't know how to respond to that.

After a few moments of silence, Rowan changed the subject, seeming to pick up on Nolan's confusion. "Well, I have faith you'll be able to find your way. Are you a fan of cards?" Rowan pulled a deck out of his small bag.

"Uh, sure. What game?"

As Rowan dealt out the cards, Nolan watched him, still perplexed at the whole situation. This guy had come to check on him, to see how he was doing. How he was feeling. Who does that for someone they'd only met once?

That made Nolan think of Rowan's last point: "How can you decide something when you don't know how you feel about it?"

Nolan wasn't particularly in touch with his feelings. His folks had always been more focused on analyzing a problem rather than relying on your gut. But is that what was missing? Is that what had driven Tori away?

What he wouldn't give to be able to know.

THE LASTING IMPACT OF SUPPORT

Over the next few days, Nolan had more visitors than he knew what to do with. Callie and Kenta had played cards with him, Tate had watched a basketball game with him, and Rowan talked with him. They made the time fly by until Nolan was ready to be released— and to his surprise, Rowan and Mia offered to help him get home.

As the three of them pulled into the parking lot at Nolan's apartment complex, Nolan could feel his nerves start to act up. "Well, thanks again for the ride! I really appreciate it," he said as he tried to wrangle his crutches and legs out of the car.

"Can't we help you get settled?" Rowan asked.

"I'm..." Before he could finish his sentence, Nolan put too much pressure on his bad ankle and winced in pain.

"Okay, we're helping you in," Mia said.

Nolan sighed, knowing she was right. He needed the help.

After he unlocked and opened the door, a pungent smell emerged from the apartment. Mia scrunched up her nose. "What is *that?*"

Nolan was horrified; he had forgotten how bad he'd let the place get. As Rowan helped Nolan lie down on the couch, he could see Mia surveying the room, her face a strange mix of emotions. Once Nolan was settled, Rowan and Mia stepped into the chaotic kitchen and had a hushed conversation.

Hearing their whispering, Nolan's embarrassment rose. He wished he could just send them away and not have to deal with their judgment, but he didn't want to offend them after all they'd done for him. He tried to pick up a few wrappers from the coffee table, then realized he didn't have anywhere to put them.

Suddenly the conversation ended, and the pair walked over to Nolan. "Do you mind if we tidy up a bit while we wait for Tate?" Rowan asked.

"Tate?" Nolan asked.

"Yeah, he's going to stop by with some groceries to make breakfast," Mia said.

"I'm not sure about all this..."

"If you want us to leave, just say it," Mia said.

Man, she didn't mince her words. Nolan really respected that about Mia; he could never *just say* what he was thinking. "Actually, it's fine... for just a bit."

"Wonderful," Rowan said with a smile.

Mia and Rowan each took a position. Mia grabbed a trash bag to clear spoiled foods out of the fridge, while Rowan tackled the overflowing garbage island.

Before long, there was a knock at the door. *That must be Tate,* Nolan thought.

But instead, when Rowan opened the door, in bopped Amani in tennis clothing. "Hi Nolan!" she greeted him before walking over to Mia.

"Nice skirt," Mia teased.

"Actually, it's a *skort,* thank you very much," Amani responded, doing a quick curtsy.

Mia snorted loudly and nodded in approval.

"I've gotten back into playing lately. I'm really making an effort to do more things for myself," Amani said, a humble smile on her face. "But anyway, what can I help with?" Amani answered her own question by scrounging up some cleaning spray and a rag.

"This is a cute photo," Mia said, looking at a picture stuck to the fridge. "Who's she?"

"That's Tori, my girlfriend," Nolan said, smiling for the first time all day.

"Oh, I didn't realize you had a girlfriend," Mia said.

Nolan's face fell. He couldn't believe he'd just called her his girlfriend. He knew better than that.

"Um, actually we broke up. So, *ex*-girlfriend."

"Why'd you break up?" Mia asked in her typical filter-less way.

Because I can't ever make a decision. Because she couldn't go on dating someone who can't think for himself, Nolan thought. But he didn't say anything. His throat started to go dry, and he could feel his upper lip forming sweat droplets. How could he explain what had happened?

Nolan was saved by a crashing sound.

"You were a little short," Rowan said to Mia with a hearty laugh.

Mia looked over at Nolan's confused face. "I tried to throw this tuna can into your trash can, and I missed, okay?" she said defensively. She turned to Rowan. "I was just trying to get some practice in!"

Another knock at the door cut off Rowan's response. "Look who I found in the parking lot!" Kenta said, dropping a bag of groceries on the counter as Tate walked in behind him.

"Thank god you did, I wouldn't have been able to carry this all up by myself," Tate said, huffing a little from the walk up. "I figured your fridge was probably pretty empty, so I brought a few extra things."

Amani emerged from the bathroom. "We gotta get you some new toilet cleaner, hun! I just used the last of yours."

Now they were cleaning his *bathroom?* Nolan suddenly felt overwhelmed by their generosity. How was he going to pay them back? Should he tell them to stop? Would that come off as ungrateful?

Rowan saw Nolan's eyes darting around the room and sat down in the chair next to him.

"You know," Nolan said quietly to Rowan. "I think I'm good. You guys are free to leave."

"Is that really what you want? To clean all this up by yourself—and on your crutches?" Rowan asked.

Nolan hemmed and hawed. No, he didn't want to clean this up while hobbling around. But it was his mess. Shouldn't he be the one cleaning it up?

"Why don't you think it over, and then let me know. We're happy to go or stay." Rowan said. "Your choice."

Nolan nodded, contemplating this.

"Rowan, can you give me a hand?" Amani yelled from the kitchen.

"Let us know, okay?" Rowan said, hopping up and hurrying off.

Nolan watched as Mia helped Kenta unload the groceries, telling him about the view from her new apartment. Next to the table, Amani giggled as she looked at her phone. "Guys, look at this picture the kids took of Biscuit. They put sunglasses on him!" she squealed, walking over to Rowan, Mia, Tate, and Kenta.

Nolan smiled, watching the happy frenzy unfold before him.

"You have a frying pan somewhere around here?" Kenta asked, opening a cupboard.

Nolan took that as his cue to finally get up. He grabbed his crutches and propped himself up on them carefully. He could feel that everyone had stopped what they were doing, and a dozen eyes were watching him.

"It's over in this cupboard," Nolan said, pointing. "What are you making? I'd love to help," he said, giving Rowan a nod.

Rowan smiled, nodding in return. "Let's get this food cooking!"

Soon, the sizzle of bacon filled the room, and everyone had to practically yell to be heard over the exhaust fan.

Someone else knocked on the door. "I'll get it," Nolan offered since he was already up. It was Callie, holding a bag.

"Nolan! You're looking great!" she squealed. "Amani texted

that you needed some more cleaning stuff, so I just wanted to drop this off." Callie stuck her head in the apartment. "Hey y'all!"

"Callie!" everyone exclaimed.

"I gotta go pick up Liam from his swim class, but I'll see you all soon! Much love!"

Before she turned around, she gave Nolan another look. Then, she squeezed his shoulders. "So glad to see you home safe." With that, she was gone, and Nolan was left holding a bag full of cleaning products and sponges.

The next hours seemed to fly by. They cooked up omelets, bacon, toast, and hashbrowns. They crowded around Nolan's small kitchen table and talked about all subjects under the sun.

Through it all, Nolan sat, quiet for the most part, and observed the amazing dynamic among the Crew and what each person brought to the table. There was Mia with her alarming frankness, which always cut through any front someone was putting on. Amani was the mother hen, making sure everyone was taken care of. Kenta had a gentle kindness to him, and he helped out however he could. Tate was a little more reserved than the others, but he worked hard at whatever he was doing. Callie, though not present now, had a shining, joyful energy about her.

Then there was Rowan. Nolan could see that Rowan was the head of this chosen family—not by decree, but because everyone treated him with such respect. He exuded this relaxed demeanor that calmed Nolan down just by being around him. Nolan found himself wondering how this group of people from so many different walks of life had gotten to be so close.

All too soon, mealtime was over and cleanup began. Then that was over too, and one by one his newfound friends headed out. The last one at the door was Amani.

"What are you doing tomorrow?" Amani asked.

Nolan shrugged. "Just work. Why?"

"Our group hangs out on Monday evenings at The Hearth. We do a lot of different things. Sometimes we just talk, sometimes we meditate, sometimes we journal, sometimes we dance. It's a kind of self-care time for all of us. I'd love it if you'd join us tomorrow."

"Oh, um..."

To go or not to go? Nolan's mind was racing with uncertainty. *But these people had all given their morning to help. What was there to even consider?*

"I'd love to," Nolan said.

"Wonderful! I can pick you up at quarter to seven, if that works?" Amani asked.

"Sounds great," Nolan agreed.

After saying goodbye and closing the door, Nolan's apartment seemed so... quiet. Nolan crutched his way across his newly tidied apartment and notice how good that felt, even though his leg was throbbing.

Did that all just really happen? But as he looked around at the sparkling apartment, he knew his eyes weren't deceiving him. Nolan found himself feeling cared for and thinking about tomorrow—and really looking forward to it. It felt good to make plans again.

It felt good to *decide* to make plans again.

Feeling empowered, he went with that energy. He pulled his phone out of his pocket and opened his mom's contact.

Just wanted you to know that I fell playing basketball and hurt my ankle. But I'm okay. I'll tell you more about it next time I see you.

Hitting the send arrow, he put his phone down and closed his eyes. He'd earned a moment to relax.

TAPPING INTO RESILIENCE

Even though Nolan had been feeling confident about his decision to go to The Hearth, by the time he actually pulled into the parking lot with Amani, those familiar nerves started spreading. Was he spending too much time with this group of people? Should he be at home resting instead? What if his cast didn't fit under the table? Would they have to reconfigure everything for him?

Nolan didn't move for a few moments after Amani had parked. He was staring off into the distance when a tap on his shoulder launched him back into reality.

"Gonna be hard to eat in the car," Amani joked.

"Oh sorry, I was just thinking," Nolan said, gathering his crutches.

"Mmm. You seem to do that a lot," Amani said as they walked toward the restaurant. An eruption of greetings exploded from around the room as they walked in.

"So glad you could make it, Nolan!" Callie exclaimed.

"How are you feeling?" Tate asked as he set the table.

"Oh, I'm fine," Nolan said.

Smirks emerged from around the room. "We don't love 'fine' as an answer to how you're doing," Mia said. "It doesn't really say much about what's going on."

"Um, I don't really know what else to say?" Nolan said. He looked around, confused.

"It doesn't matter. We're just thrilled you're here," Rowan said.

As they caught up, the Crew were soon enjoying a meal around one of the large, round tables at The Hearth. They all looked back at Nolan with wide smiles—even Mia, who seemed more jovial than usual. As five excited faces looked back at Nolan, he could feel his own mood shifting to match theirs.

They chatted between bites of their tacos and enchiladas. "I realized that there's still so much about you that we don't know, Nolan!" Amani said between crunchy bites. "So, tell us more about you. What's something you've done that you're proud of?"

"Something I'm proud of?"

Amani nodded, and everyone else patiently waited for an answer.

"Oh um..." Nolan rarely felt proud of himself. It felt like such an odd question to even be asked. So, he picked the most obvious answer. "Well, I graduated from college."

"*Avive la vie!*" everyone yelled, throwing up their hands in celebration. The shock of it made Nolan smile.

"That's definitely something to be proud of!" Callie said. "What'd you major in?"

"Accounting. Well, I double majored, actually. Couldn't choose just one, so I went with two polar opposites. Go figure," he huffed. "You'll laugh, but archaeology was the other one. I secretly wanted to discover the next big shipwreck." Nolan shook his head. "Kind of embarrassing when I think back to it now."

"Um, that sounds badass to me," Mia declared, wiping sour cream off her cheek. "Why would it be embarrassing?"

"I don't know. I just haven't done anything with it, so, kind of a waste of money."

Kenta chimed in, "I think it's impressive you majored in it at all. My parents totally pushed me away from studying what I wanted to. It takes a lot of guts to go after what you want, especially at eighteen."

"Thanks, that's a nicer way to look at it," Nolan said.

"I actually went to an archeology camp in school," Rowan said. "But then we got in trouble for using the geodes as ammo for our slingshots."

"Seriously?" Mia asked with a laugh.

"Oh yeah! I'm amazed we all got out with both eyes!" Rowan started laughing heartily, and his joy spread around the table.

"I know what you mean," Nolan said. "I built a catapult for a competition in high school, and that thing could do some damage!"

"A catapult! How big was it?" Amani asked.

"Oh, maybe four feet long? It was sizeable, for sure." Nolan chuckled. "It had to move forward six feet, and then shoot a ball at this little target across the room. We had such a blast building it. It kept falling apart and missing its shot. But on the day of the competition, it was perfect, and we ended up winning the whole thing."

"*Avive la vie!*" again the group cheered.

"I didn't even know they had contests for that sort of thing!" Callie said giddily. "That's amazing!"

"That was in school? Or you made it at home?" Rowan asked.

"It was in shop class. One of the only electives I took, actually."

As Nolan was saying this, he could feel the same joy and pride he had felt in his body on that competition day. He had taken shop because it was something he was interested in. It was one of the few times he had made a decision that he'd actually felt good about.

"Did you build it by yourself?" Kenta asked.

"No," Nolan said, his face falling. "I didn't." A wave of grief crashed over him; grief he hadn't thought about in a very long time.

"Everything okay, Nolan?" Kenta asked quietly.

"Yeah... yeah. I built it with my friend Jamal," Nolan said softly.

"Are you still friends with Jamal?" Mia asked, more gently than normal.

"No, um, he was in a car accident when we were juniors. He... didn't make it." Nolan clenched his jaw, trying to hold back the sorrow flooding over him.

"Oh my god," Callie whispered, tears already filling her eyes.

"I was actually supposed to be with him, in the car. But I was having fun at our friend's house and told him I'd catch a ride with someone else. Maybe if I hadn't..." Nolan looked down, unable to finish the sentence.

Everyone sat silently as the heavy words lingered in the air.

"I can't imagine that kind of loss, for you or his parents. That's just unthinkable," Amani said.

"Yeah, they were pretty heartbroken." Nolan was surprised he was even talking about this. But it felt natural, which in itself was strange. "I was pretty close with his folks because I spent a decade hanging out at their house. So, I tried to do what I could to help them. For a long time, I'd still go over for Friday night dinners, just like I used to do." Nolan sighed, looking down at the table. "I haven't talked to them in a few years. I should reach out."

"That's pretty amazing you did that as a teenager, Nolan," Kenta said quietly.

"That says a lot about you," Rowan added.

Nolan shrugged. "I think anyone would have done that in my position."

"No," Amani said. "They wouldn't have."

"Well, thanks, that's nice of you all to say," Nolan said, clearing his throat in hopes of hiding the quiver in his voice.

Amani could see his emotions beginning to surface. "Nolan, will you do something for me? Will you stand up and just listen? There's something we want your body to hear."

"Um, okay." It was a strange request, but Nolan had spent enough time with the Crew to know there was a good purpose behind it. He grabbed his crutches and awkwardly stood up.

Kenta put his food down, wiping his hands on his napkin, before turning to look up at Nolan. "I still can't get over how you went to your friend's parents' house every week. That takes some real maturity and kindness, even for adults."

Nolan nodded slightly in thanks, rocking back and forth on his crutches uncomfortably.

"And can we talk about your creativity? Who builds a moving catapult that wins awards?" Callie exclaimed, smiling at Nolan.

"I mean, I'll forever think of you as way cooler for studying bones and treasure. You've got to have a sense of adventure to even be interested in that," Mia said.

"And a drive to pursue that passion in school," Rowan added.

"And you're so humble on top of all that," Amani said.

Nolan stood, uncomfortably swaying as he listened. All these genuine truths about him at once were overwhelming. "All right, all right. That's enough," he said, waving his hands. "Thank you."

Amani caught Nolan's gaze. "You did graduate from college, right?" she asked.

"Yeah."

"And you built a catapult that won a competition?"

Nolan took a deep breath. "Yeah."

"And you kept visiting Jamal's parents after his death?"

Nolan couldn't respond. All he could picture was sitting at their dining table, making small talk, while Jamal's chair sat empty across from him.

"Nolan?" Kenta asked, snapping Nolan out of it.

"Everything we're saying is true, Nolan. It's not subjective, or biased. *You* made these decisions. *You* did these things. It's just the truth," Rowan said.

This was too much. Nolan couldn't take it anymore.

"Sorry, I gotta get some air." Nolan made his way to the front door as quickly as he could. As soon as he got outside, he took a deep inhale of the cool night air. He kept breathing, trying to quiet the flurry of thoughts going through in his mind. After a few minutes, Mia came out to join him.

"Why are you guys saying all that? That I'm creative and brave. It's not true." Nolan said.

"We were just going off what you were telling us," she said with a shrug, moving to stand beside him.

He shook his head. "I can't make decisions to save my life. Those were just random things I did. They don't mean anything."

"So, someone else made those choices for you? Someone held you at gunpoint and made you an archaeology major?" Mia said.

He let out a short laugh. "Of course not."

"Yeah, thought so. You know, inside there, we're having dinner with this pretty cool dude. He looks out for other people, builds cool stuff. Doesn't suck at basketball. I think you'd like him."

With that, she gave Nolan a light pat on the back and walked back into the restaurant, leaving Nolan alone with his thoughts.

Nolan took a deep breath as he thought about what Mia had said. Did they really think he was a "pretty cool dude"? He did build that catapult, after all; that was pretty cool. And he had always been a big fan of archaeology. Was that interesting?

After wallowing in self-pity for so many days, it was almost a shock to the system to think he might *not* be such a hopeless failure after all.

Nolan began thinking back on his dinners with Jamal's parents. He hadn't thought about them in so long. It felt good to remember their gratitude and how close he felt to them as they shared their memories of their beloved son and his best friend. As he sunk further into the memory, Nolan remembered something else: a conversation he'd had with his own parents before joining Jamal's parents for dinner for the first time after Jamal's death.

"Are you sure they're ready for visitors?" his mom had asked.

"It's so soon, maybe you should just stay home," his dad had added.

But Nolan didn't hesitate. He knew going to their house was the right thing to do, so he went without a second thought.

Without a second thought.

Nolan was almost startled by this revelation. He was capable of trusting his gut, of knowing the right choice to make. Maybe he just needed to trust that part of himself more.

Nolan straightened himself up, a little taller than before. He'd had enough self-doubt for tonight. He was going to go back inside and enjoy himself.

Opening the door, Nolan was met with a wall of laughter. The group had moved on to another topic. They weren't waiting with a pity party, or awkwardly trying to ignore what had just happened. They were joyfully present in the moment, going with whatever was coming up, and the whole space was filled with the warmth of people truly connecting with one another.

"Hey, there's the catapult builder!" Callie announced.

Nolan smiled sheepishly and waved. "Thanks again for all that. It meant a lot." As Nolan looked at each of these people, he genuinely felt like they all cared for him.

"Anytime, bud," Mia said. "Also, do you still remember how to build that catapult? That sounds like an awesome weekend project." And just like that, the conversation veered toward building and making, and what projects they could create together.

A MOMENT IN THE MIRROR: OVERWHELMED BY SELF-DOUBT

Within yourself, can you recognize Nolan's False Belonging Habit: **I believe if I make the "right" decision, regardless of what I actually think, I will belong.**

We've all weighed the pros and cons of monumental life decisions like moving, getting a new job, or making a major purchase. And we've all experienced self-doubt when trying to figure out the best way to move forward. Taking a pause before choosing something isn't a bad thing, but when that pause lasts so long that we don't actually come to a decision, we get into dangerous territory.

For some of us, like Nolan, self-doubt is frequent and, sometimes, debilitating. This doubt can show up every day, within nearly every decision we try to make. Even more, some of us are plagued by needing to make the "right" call (based on others' opinions), even if it's not what our heart is telling us.

Let's see how much self-doubt plays a role in your life. Try to trust your initial response to each question.

1. Does it take you a long time to write a text or email because you keep erasing and rewriting?
2. Do you let others talk over you or speak for you because you're unsure of yourself?
3. Do you answer questions with other questions to avoid committing yourself to an answer?
4. Do you find yourself giving mixed messages?
5. When you make a decision, do you feel overwhelmed or second-guess yourself?
6. Do you have a hard time identifying your feelings and putting them into words?

We've witnessed how each Crew member's False Belonging Habit had a good intention—to belong—and also how that intention didn't translate to *actual* belonging. Let's see what their lives look like after they've gone through this transformation.

CHAPTER 8

COMING TOGETHER

Rowan pulled his mother's wheelchair out of the back of the car, then pushed it over to the passenger door. "Ready?" he asked.

"As I'll ever be," she answered with a smile. This wheelchair was relatively new, and Rowan still found it strange to have to help his mom around like this. She'd always been so independent and strong; he didn't quite know what to do with this new version of her.

As he helped his mother down, Rowan could already hear the sounds of the fundraiser from the parking lot.

"Do you mind if we go for a walk down by the creek before we go over?" Rowan's mother asked, now securely in her chair.

"Sure thing." Rowan started pushing her down the path, skirting the edge of the event they would be attending. Before long, they reached a bench in the shade of a grand oak tree.

"This is good," she said. "Why don't you take a seat?"

"That sounds quite ominous," Rowan joked, parking his mother next to the bench before he sat down.

She inhaled deeply, closing her eyes. Rowan watched as she exhaled and relaxed her shoulders.

"I got a call from Dr. Roberts today. They got the biopsy back. It's stage four."

Rowan's head dropped as he let this sink in. "Okay. So, what does he suggest for the next treatment plan?"

"There isn't another treatment plan, Ro Ro. It seems we've reached my swan song."

Rowan's head snapped over to look at his mother. She had said it so calmly, so matter-of-factly, but it couldn't be true.

"Well, if he doesn't have one, there are other doctors we can see."

Rowan's mother waved her hand. "Not this time, honey. I'm tired. I've lived a long life. It's my time."

Rowan shook his head emphatically. "No," he whispered, hot tears filling his eyes. His lungs felt weighted down as the sobs started surging through his body.

"Come here," his mother said, wrapping her arms around her son as he laid his head on her shoulder.

They sat like this for quite some time. At first the sorrow was so acute that Rowan would physically shake with each sob. As he did, his mother held him tighter. Then Rowan felt the pain lightening. He opened his eyes, his head still on her shoulder, and watched the creek flowing slowly by. He watched a duck floating downstream, his little head dipping under the water to look for food.

Then Rowan looked up to the sky, its light blue hue masked by the leafy tree branches above him.

He felt his head lift as his mother inhaled. He glanced up at her. He had always loved watching her breathe. She seemed to be so conscious about every inhale and exhale—like she knew the power they wielded. And right now, she seemed as calm as ever.

But soon, Rowan realized, he wouldn't be able to experience that anymore. He wouldn't be able to experience anything about her anymore.

And just like that, the anguish was back. Rowan wept, turning in closer to his mother. Now, her palm rested on the crown of his head, stroking his hair. Despite everything he was feeling, this simple gesture offered so much comfort.

After a while more, the tears lost their force. Rowan managed to get in a deep breath and sat up slowly. His mother reached around in her purse and pulled out a tissue for her son.

She waited a few moments, looking out over the water. Then she said, "You know what's interesting? Now that I know it's coming, I find myself replaying all these wonderful moments from my life. Many of those involve you, you know," she said, patting his leg.

"Well, you've got a lot to choose from," Rowan said, his voice still shaky.

"Mmm. But my memory isn't what it used to be. Can you help me fill in a gap that's been bothering me?"

"Of course."

"Remember when we went to that talent show where Pierre sang?"

Rowan let out a laugh. "Oh yeah! I remember everyone was so surprised to see that big guy with all the tattoos singing a song in French."

"That's my question. What song did he sing?"

"Oh, what was it called… he used to sing it all the time." Rowan snapped his fingers when it came to him. "*Ne me quitte pas!*"

His mom clapped in delight. "That was it! Oh, thank you." She smiled. "He did such a beautiful job! And he was so proud. It was such a wonderful night."

"You helped him be able to do that, you know," Rowan said, with a nod toward her.

"I'd say we both did. He lived with us for, what, six months? You two formed quite a bond. I think that helped with his confidence."

Rowan smiled at the memory. "Remember how reserved he was at first? He was so self-conscious about his English. He was so hesitant to even come stay with us at all. He still had those big bandages around his wrists when you first brought him home from the hospital. And there I was, bouncing off the walls with that huge cast from breaking my arm. I don't think he wanted anything to do with me at first."

His mother laughed. "I think it was just what he needed." She smiled warmly. "He really did blossom, didn't he? He went from barely saying two words to always singing or humming and celebrating every moment. And that's when we finally got to hear 'Vive la vie!'"

"'Live life to the fullest.' That phrase was the biggest gift he could have given us, honestly," Rowan said. He paused. "How did it turn into 'UH-veev la vee'?"

"You don't remember?" his mother asked. "You had a little trouble with the French pronunciation, so you just threw an 'a' on the front. I always loved how you put your own special twist on it."

"Why didn't you ever correct me?" Rowan asked.

His mom looked at him, her eyes crinkling up from her smile. "Why would I do that? Your version was perfect."

At this, a new wave of heartbreak spread through his chest.

She took his hand in hers as Rowan let this wave of grief work its way through him. She didn't try to rush him or say anything to change how he was feeling. She simply sat and held space for her beloved son.

Before long, the wave had moved on, and Rowan was drying his cheeks.

"That's the beauty of *Avive la vie*, Ro Ro. It's not just a celebration. It's a celebration of life, connection, and belonging. And whenever you say it or see it or feel it, you'll still be connected to me." She took a deep breath. "I like to think that that's my legacy. And I know you'll continue it. You already are."

As Rowan contemplated this idea, he heard footsteps behind him.

"There you two are! We need to make a few last decisions before we get up and running. Mind if I steal you away?" a man from the fundraiser asked Rowan's mother.

She looked over at Rowan, who gave a nod.

"Yes, let's go. I'll catch up with you later, hun."

As the two disappeared up the path, Rowan sat, almost in a daze. His body felt overloaded, like he couldn't fully process what he'd heard. He knew he needed to get up, to help with the event, but his legs didn't seem to work. So, he looked around once again at the dragonfly buzzing by the tall grass. The rock sticking up just above the water. The dark, fuzzy moss growing on the bark of a tree. Yes, he was in pain, but he could also enjoy this moment. This fundraiser meant so much to his mom, and him, so he could still try to soak up the joy of the day.

Rowan finally got his legs to comply and stood up. He walked up a different path, this one leading straight to the property. People were already buzzing around, putting the final pieces together before the fundraiser fully opened.

The event was the annual fundraiser for a nonprofit Rowan's mother had long been on the board of. There were rows of tiny houses on the property which provided temporary homes for the unhoused. Rowan could see the brightly colored front doors from where he stood in the large, open, grassy space where they hosted the event.

Rowan walked toward the food booth, where he could already smell the scent of grilled burgers and veggie hot dogs. "There he is!" Kenta said as Rowan approached.

"How's it going over here?" Rowan asked.

"Just peachy," Mia said, pulling buns out of a box.

"Should be ready to go in no time," Sydney said as she got the cash drawer set up.

"Wonderful. Thanks again for helping out," Rowan said. Mia stopped what she was doing and looked at him. Rowan was sure that she could sense something was off.

Before she could say anything, another set of volunteers walked up. "Reporting for duty!"

Rowan turned around to see not only Kenta's mother, but also his father.

"Mom! *And* Dad!" Kenta said, clearly surprised. "So glad you could come today!"

"Well, you're clearly in need of some help," his father said.

His mother hit her husband jokingly. "We're happy to be here."

Kenta thought for a moment. "I think I'm gonna have you take orders, Mom. And Dad, I'll have you prep here next to me..."

Kenta's dad cut in. "So what's on the menu? New York strip and mahi mahi?"

Kenta let out a laugh. "No, just hot dogs and burgers. It's a backyard fundraiser after all."

"I didn't know if backyard food was 'beneath' you now."

The sarcasm in his father's voice was sharp, and Rowan watched as Kenta inhaled deeply, centering himself before responding. But before he could, Mia leaned over. "Burgers are an art, Mr. Tanaka. Don't be surprised if it's the best burger you've ever seen."

Kenta smiled. "I'm just thankful you're here, Dad. I've missed you."

Kenta's father ignored his sentiment as Mia led his mother to her position. Rowan busied himself pulling out the rest of the supplies next to Kenta and his dad.

"So, Becca has really been stepping up at the firm since you left," Kenta's father said to him as he straightened up the utensils in his station.

"Oh? That's great to hear," Kenta responded.

"You know that account you'd been trying to get for years? The Duncans? She hooked 'em after two meetings."

Kenta nodded, focusing his attention on the sizzling hamburgers. "That's awesome."

"She's a powerhouse. The best junior partner I think we've ever had."

Rowan watched as Kenta inhaled and held the breath for several seconds. After he exhaled, he said, "Dad, let's forget about Becca for a second. Can I check in with you?"

Kenta's dad looked confused. "What do you mean?"

"When you keep bringing up Becca, I keep replaying this story that I'm not good enough. I know that's not true—well, now I do anyway," Kenta said, nodding to himself. Kenta looked back at this father. "I know I left the firm, but I'm still your son, you know?"

Rowan could see Mr. Tanaka tense up. He clearly didn't expect to have this conversation.

Kenta looked at the grill, choosing his words carefully. "Our relationship is one of the most important things to me, Dad. What I do for work doesn't change that. I still want to you to be a part of my life."

Now Kenta's father looked down at the table, fiddling with the tub of sliced onions.

"So today, all I want is to cook some good food with my dad for a good cause. Can we do that?"

Kenta's father finally looked over to him. "Yes, I can do that," he said with an unexpected gentleness.

Kenta grinned, his shoulders relaxing. "Great. Now, let me show you this mushroom gorgonzola sauce that's going to go on top."

Rowan focused on slicing up the last of the tomatoes, a smile on his own face. It was so inspiring to see how much Kenta had grown since Rowan first met him at that gallery. He was so sure of himself, and he prioritized connection so naturally now.

As he experienced this warmth, Rowan's mother's words rang in his head: "Whenever you say '*Avive la vie*' or see it or feel it, you'll still be connected to me." *Is this what she meant?* Rowan wondered.

He needed to clear his head. "Hey guys, I'll be back in a minute."

"Roger that!" Sydney replied as the first guests started walking over to order food.

With each step, Rowan's feet felt heavier. The more Rowan thought about his mother and everything she'd taught him about connection, the more grief he felt.

Rowan found an empty seat under a tree and sat down. The tears flowed again, just as freely as they had earlier. A few attendees looked over at Rowan with worried or concerned looks, but Rowan didn't mind. He let it out until he didn't have anything left to let out. As he wiped his eyes, he leaned his head back, looking up at the blue sky through the tree branches.

When he brought his head back down, Rowan really took in the event for the first time. There was a cotton candy machine under a tent, and a volunteer was handing out the fluffy pink spun sugar to a child. Rowan could hear the child giggling from where he sat.

Then there was the stage, which would host a local band later in the day. A few of the residents were helping the tech lead with some of the cords and cables. One of them spotted Rowan looking over and gave him a big wave.

Rowan smiled and reciprocated with a small wave. He didn't have the energy for anything bigger.

His eyes continued to scan the event. There were quite a few people coming in now. Some carried picnic blankets and folding chairs, while others held the arm of their partner or the hand of their child. But no matter what each person was doing, Rowan spotted the same thing.

Connection.

He watched as a family walked past a tent with chairs set up. Some local massage therapists had offered to gift chair massages to the unhoused and the volunteers at the event. Rowan nearly did a double take when he spotted Amani's unmistakable curly hair in one of the chairs. Amani, who couldn't even be waited on at The Hearth without wanting to help clean dishes when Rowan first met her. Amani, who felt so guilty about missing her son's soccer game that she was making herself sick.

She had finally learned to put herself on her priority list.

Again, his mother's words about connection rang through his mind. Amani had finally connected with herself. Wasn't that a form of *Avive la vie*, too?

Rowan chuckled to himself, so happy that Amani was taking some time for herself. He'd have to ask her later how the massage was. For now, he stood up, took a deep breath, and walked back to the food booth.

"Rowan, we're almost out of napkins," Mia said.

Rowan looked out at the long line of people, then back to their supply. "I have another box in my car. I'll go grab it."

Cooking duty had put the sad news about his mother out of

his mind. But as soon as he walked away from that tent, it all came flooding back. Rowan breathed through the feelings, and with each breath, the pain became less sharp.

He was okay. Everything would be okay.

As he made his way to the parking lot, Rowan's heart warmed at what a great turnout they'd had. The grassy area was full of families and couples, chatting with each other and munching down on burgers and hot dogs. With the band now playing, there was even a group dancing in front of the stage.

Rowan spotted a man spinning his young daughter around and around. He was moving so fast that Rowan couldn't see his face, but he'd recognize that baseball cap anywhere. When Tate finally stopped spinning, Rowan could make out a huge grin on his face. Witnessing the sheer joy on his friend's face, Rowan couldn't help but smile, too.

He could see Ellie jumping, clearly asking Tate for another turn. At the same time, Nadia pushed herself closer, vying for her own chance to dance with her father. Molly put her arms around her girls, her back to Rowan. Whatever she said to Tate made his smile even brighter.

Rowan couldn't help but chuckle to himself. His mom was right. *Avive la vie* was everywhere. This celebration of life and connection was all around him. And because of that, a part of his mother always would be too.

He nodded to himself and continued his walk to get the napkins. His friends were depending on him after all.

After a successful event and an hour of cleanup, everyone was sitting around the roaring bonfire. Callie was helping Liam hold his marshmallow-bearing stick over the fire. "Whoa, let's hold that up a little higher!" Callie instructed as the stick dipped a little too close to the flames.

Mia and Sydney were holding hands, chatting with Nolan and his new girlfriend, Chloe.

"Don't let him fool ya. He'll say he's not good at something, and then swoop in and land like four three-pointers," Mia joked.

Kenta and his parents were talking with Amani, who was munching on some cotton candy. "That one," Amani said, motioning to her son, "would love to climb trees and then tell no one where he was. We'd be in the park for an hour, yelling 'LUKE' straight up into the sky!"

They all laughed, and Kenta's mother said, "Well, Kenta here decided that it was a good idea to swim in a lake… in February!"

"What?!" Amani said as her jaw dropped.

"To be fair," Kenta cut in, laughing, "I think it was actually April!"

Tate and Molly had their lawn chairs pushed up next to each other and were quietly cuddling. On the grass in front of them sat their daughters. Nadia was playing a game of Crazy Eights with Luke while Ellie looked back at Rowan's mother, who sat behind her. "Do you want me to make you a s'more? Mine are really good, I promise," she said.

"You know, that does sound lovely…" Rowan's mother began.

"No, no, no!" Callie squealed. Everyone looked over to see Callie's marshmallow separating from the stick, its white gooey strand becoming longer by the second.

"If I rotate it…" Callie said, but it was too late. The marshmallow dropped into the fire.

Everyone sat for a moment, silent. Then, Liam let out a cheer: "*Avive la vie!*"

Everyone laughed and echoed him. *"Avive la vie!"*

As Liam scampered off to get another marshmallow, Rowan's mother caught her son's eye and winked.

Mia stood up then, taking a shaky breath. "Speaking of *Avive la vie...*" she took Sydney's hand and had her stand up next to her. "We, um, have some news. But everyone's got to promise not to get all lovey-dovey."

Sydney rolled her eyes playfully. "Just tell them."

Mia held up Sydney's left hand and turned it to reveal a ring. "We're engaged!"

"Show them your ring, too!" Sydney said, reaching over to hold up Mia's hand.

Rowan heard the hoots and hollers erupting around him, but he was focused only on the happy couple. Out of the corner of his eye, Rowan saw Callie jump up, the tears already streaming as she ran to look at the rings. The rest of the Crew got to their feet, eager to congratulate the newly engaged.

But Rowan just watched. He hadn't said much this evening; his heart felt so full yet heavy at the same time. He simply sat in awe of this beautiful community he was a part of.

Mia accepted the hugs and congratulations, clearly getting a little overwhelmed by all the affection. Then she finally met Rowan's gaze. Her eyes started welling up. She gave him a nod, but Rowan knew it meant so much more.

He stood up and walked over to her. He bent down to her eye level, grasping the sides of her shoulders. *"Avive la vie,"* he whispered.

Mia lunged forward, wrapping him in the tightest embrace. Rowan closed his eyes and hugged back. Then, looking back at his mom, he repeated the phrase to himself one more time.

"Avive la vie."

PART 2
THE TOOLS OF BELONGING

CHAPTER 9

CULTIVATING A CONNECTION-FIRST EXPERIENCE

A*vive la Vie* means many things. It's a celebration of life, a symbol of community, a call of connection. More than anything, it's a way of living that utilizes connection to fundamentally shift how you experience yourself and the world around you.

At this stage in the book, you've had a chance to see what a life of *Avive la Vie* did for the Crew's lives; how they were able to repair relationships, attune to themselves, and pursue the things that fulfilled and empowered them.

But before any of that could happen, the Crew had to recognize how they were habitually experiencing themselves through their False Belonging Habits. For example, Nolan thought he was indecisive while Callie thought she was too emotional. After following these Habits for so long, the two of them began to have distorted views of who they each were, becoming disconnected from the true source of their belonging.

This happens to most of us. We can get so caught up in our False Belonging Habits that it becomes hard to see our beautiful essence.

The Crew didn't need to change or fix themselves to shift their lives. Neither do you. To move into *Avive la Vie*—a life focused on connection first—we begin by looking inward for the core aspects of our being which help us realize the truth of who we are: love-able, valuable, and connected. We do not need to gain these elements or build them up, because they are already within each and every one of us.

The first step to accessing these parts of ourselves is dismantling our False Belonging Habits, including our patterns of fearing vulnerability and risking rejection. We'll demonstrate how reconnecting with our emotional body allows us to break out of our self-destructive cycle, as well as the cost if we don't. Next, we'll investigate how to respond to anxiety-inducing situations in a way that keeps us focused on connection rather than our conditioned thoughts. Finally, after showing you how to do all this on your own, you'll learn how you can begin to involve your loved ones in this wonderful, connection-first way of life.

None of these ideas are overly complicated or difficult; this is an introduction to these concepts rather than a step-by-step guide. The invitation now is to open your heart and mind to the essential first steps: recognizing that you are innately embedded with love and value.

CONNECTING WITH YOUR TRUE SELF

To begin living a life of *Avive la Vie*, we must tap into two buried aspects of ourselves that are a crucial part of who we are as human beings: our innate love and value.

The value of who you are is fundamental, inborn, inherent, and natural. Similarly, the love that exists within you is permanent, real, essential, and unquestionable. However, our sense of connection to our innate love and value has been through the wringer, much like our sense of belonging. The reason comes back, once again, to the correction-first way many of us were raised and have lived our lives.

At this point, we know that our False Belonging Habits led us to believe that we often had to *do* something to earn our belonging, whether that was performing (Kenta), caring for others (Amani), or reserving our emotions (Callie). And much of the time, we looked to others to determine if what we did was acceptable enough to belong.

If Kenta's colleagues liked his work, he believed he belonged.

If Amani's kids felt cared for, she believed she belonged.

If no one poked fun at Callie, she believed she belonged.

All of these fixes were just temporary, though. These feelings of belonging only lasted through that one event. Once the moment passed, the sense of belonging disappeared, and it had to be earned all over again.

Just as these three let others determine if they belonged, they also depended on others to tell them how valuable and lovable they were.

Kenta felt valuable when he won a design bid.

Amani felt loved when she was thanked for going above and beyond.

Callie felt safe when others didn't comment on her emotions.

The Crew didn't consciously *decide* to outsource their sense of love and value to others, and neither do we. Making decisions or taking actions based on our conditioning isn't something we do consciously. It just happens, over and over again, until we end up believing our conditioning is who we really are.

Does this mean you *never* experience your innate love and value until you achieve this new awareness and release all of your funky old habits? Of course not! It simply means that when you are experiencing a ton of anxiety or self-doubt, you will find it harder, much harder, to connect with your innate goodness and inherent wholeness.

When we learn to connect to these inherent aspects of ourselves, like the Crew did, we no longer look to the outside world to determine who we are. We no longer search for our sense of belonging outwardly or question if we belong. This deep sense of love and value is truly the definition of belonging: belonging with *ourselves*.

It's an interesting idea, isn't it? Belonging with ourselves? Just as our connections with others are important and life-giving, our deep sense of belonging in our own bones deserves our attention.

When we embody our innate love and value, we can fully experience true belonging with ourselves. And from this point, we can extend that belonging to include other people in our lives. So, let's dive into experiencing one of the foundational pieces of belonging: innate value.

EXPERIENCING YOUR INNATE VALUE

Picture a sweet, laughing, six-month-old baby. Would you say this baby is valuable?

What a question, right? Of course this baby is valuable! It's a living, breathing, wondrous being with countless possibilities for whom they will grow up to be.

But what happens when we hold this baby to the standards that many of us have for ourselves—the standards we've come up with for what makes us "valuable?"

Is the baby contributing to society? No, they are completely dependent on the people around them.

Is the baby always acting in the way they "should"? No, they cry and throw things.

See where we're going with this? This baby has value simply because they are alive. Period. There is nothing this baby could do to negate their own, innate value.

And the same is true for each of us. Our value is built in. No one can diminish our worth, no matter how much they may try. Even our own actions can't weaken our true value and the essence of who we are. Whether we mess up horribly or succeed beyond our wildest dreams—or even do both simultaneously—we have the exact same amount of value. And the way to access our innate value is by putting down the impossible-to-meet standards that we've been holding over our heads for so long.

These self-imposed expectations and requirements are different for each person. For Amani, she believed herself to be a valuable mother when she prioritized her family over her work, without exception. Now that you've gotten to know Amani, would you say she is less valuable for missing her son's soccer game in order to accept an incredible work opportunity? No, of course not. Her value isn't dependent on one specific situation. Even more, her value isn't dependent on *any* situation. Her value is inherent; it can never be lost or diminished.

Take a moment to consider how you measure your own worth. What are the things from your life that you think determine your value? Your performance at work? How well your kids are doing in school? The number of arguments you get into with your partner? Your pant size?

Now, think back to that drooling, crying baby. Would you ever use that same measurement to quantify the baby's value? Would you say, "If this baby spits up *this* many times, they're no longer valuable!"? Of course not.

Try on this compassionate perspective, the one you extended to the baby. Ask yourself: like this baby, do I have the right to exist? Do I value my own life?

You're here on this planet, just like that baby. So, do you have the right to live? YES!

Can you feel every emotion under the sun and be whatever you want to be? YES!

Do you have the right to be you, exactly as you are? YES!

Notice how it feels to say, "I am valuable. I AM valuable. I AM!" Can you feel the liberation of declaring your worth?

Let's use this momentum to move on to our innate love.

EXPERIENCING YOUR INNATE LOVE

Right now, in this moment, how loving do you feel? And how loveable?

Understanding innate love can be tricky because we're used to measuring love by external transactions. We often think that our lovability depends on how much others love us, and that how loving we are is determined by how successful our relationships are—how much others feel loved by us.

Innate love is our nature, immeasurable and intangible. There's no point in trying to quantify it. Love is our connection to ourselves and to all of life. Love just is, without any need for evaluation.

Innate love is our *capacity* for love—how much love we can feel in our heart—not necessarily how fully that love is shared or expressed. We talk about a "loving person" as someone who is in touch with dwelling in and sharing the warmth of compassion and heartfelt presence. But what do we really know about another person's experience? The most loving person in the room may go completely unnoticed; their heart may be full of love, but they're not outwardly sharing it.

There are so many ways we can access love—where we can truly feel that we already have this love inside us, and that you don't have to earn or gain or win love from someone else. Think back over your life. Have you had a family dog or cat or bird or lizard that you loved unconditionally? What about your closest playmate from when you were a child? Was there a kind of friendship love there?

What about an older cousin who always looked out for you? An aunt who sneaked you extra dessert? A neighbor who taught you to play cards? Do you notice a warmth building within you as you think about the positive relationships in your life—the people you connected with?

While we may feel burdened by a few exceptionally difficult relationships, or memories of love lost, we find ourselves still yearning for, striving for, and anticipating loving relationships. Experiencing our innate love is about opening our hearts again and again to feel what's already inside us, allowing us to move past heartaches and embrace new connections.

It can seem that our love comes from the people in our lives, but the truth is we must already possess the capacity to love in order to experience *being* loved. And that innate love can show up in many places in our lives.

Think of your favorite TV show. Have you grown fond of the characters? Do you feel comfortable and at ease watching the plot unfold? You've likely said, "I love this show!" Isn't this a form of love?

Do you have a hobby that warms your heart and makes you feel uplifted every time you do it? Isn't that a form of self-love?

The houseplant that has flourished because of your care. Your canine companion whom you feed every morning. Couldn't these be considered forms of love?

Take a moment and sit with this idea. Allow yourself to remember and savor all the little moments of love in your life.

We all have this ability. We naturally feel this inner love at milestones in our lives like a birth, a wedding, a dear one's sickness, a magnificent accomplishment, or even a death. Isn't that what we experienced with Rowan and his mother around the bonfire? There was an outpouring of connection, emotional sharing, and affection—a demonstration of innate love.

Do you have the capacity to love? YES!

Can you feel connected to your innate love? YES!

Notice how it feels to say to yourself, "YES! I am a loving and lovable person."

If you're having trouble connecting with your innate love and value, don't worry. Sometimes it can be hard to tap into these innate aspects of ourselves, especially when we've felt disconnected from them for so long. Give yourself some grace if your connection feels a little tenuous right now. The more you practice living in a connection-first mindset and letting go of a correction-based way of thinking, the more your innate love and value will reveal themselves to you.

TAHO: A PLACE TO CALL HOME

Imagine someone said to Superman, "Hey, you were flying way too fast!" "Your cape is looking pretty wrinkled." "You dented my car when you lifted it off that little girl!"

It's ridiculous to imagine that anyone could ignore all the amazing things Superman is doing for mankind just to nitpick him, yet this is what we do to ourselves every day. Every time we critique and criticize ourselves, we experience a kind of separation from our own internal hero: our Taho.

Taho is the embodiment of your innate value and love. When you call upon your Taho, you access the truth of who you've always been and restore the link to your innate wholeness. You powerfully feel that you belong, whether alone or with others. You *know* you belong. Some people relate to Taho as the most spiritually connected aspect of themselves, because when we're fully, totally connected to our Taho, we experience an undeniable sense of true belonging.

Unfortunately, for much of our lives, we've been led to believe that others determine if we belong or not. We feel diminished by the harsh words of others, as if we have no value in that moment. We allow them to dictate how lovable we believe we are. We learn to neglect the deep well of innate value and love that lives within us. We allow our False Belonging Habits to filter the version of ourselves that we see.

We've wasted years, decades even, nitpicking (and ignoring) ourselves in this way.

Isn't it time we tried something else?

To embrace our innate value and love—our Taho—we can learn more about the main roadblocks that stand in our way: our False Belonging Habits. While we've seen how these patterns play out in people's lives, we're going to dissect exactly what makes up this False Belonging Habit cycle. And yes, we're going to break this cycle!

To understand this, let's go back to the Crew. The consequences that came from following their Habits were evident: from Tate nearly losing his family to Mia distancing herself from Sydney and Amani almost torpedoing her career. In the real world, we all experience similar repercussions. We might not talk about a recent accomplishment because we don't want to seem vain, but then feel disheartened when no one celebrates us. We might not go out of our way to connect with a new colleague, then feel guilty when we see that person eating their lunch alone in their car. Sometimes we push our closest friends and family away in the moments we need them most, then feel completely alone in our struggles. We find ourselves deciding how "good" we are based on how well we fit the mold of who we think we should be.

So many of us have been taught that it's natural to be in a perpetual state of anxiety about needing to say the right thing or act the right way. We may believe that it's normal for others to determine how we feel about ourselves. Ultimately, we've been unconsciously living under a spell that has robbed us of our most important self-truths.

This isn't okay. It's never been okay. And it's time we lived a different way.

We've seen how it's possible to move down a different path. With the help of Rowan, the Crew were able to completely transform their attitudes, outlooks, and ultimately, their lives. They learned how connection with ourselves and others is as vital to our health and well-being as food, water, and air. They chose to prioritize fostering a true sense of belonging within themselves, rather than continue to ignore it (like so many of us do).

Most importantly, they learned how to reclaim their Taho and finally stop believing their sense of belonging is controlled by others.

Let's wake ourselves from this spell we've been sold. Let's venture forward to see how you can tap into the beauty of *Avive la Vie* in your own life. We start by going back to where we began: our False Belonging Habits.

CHAPTER 10

UNHOOKING FROM YOUR FALSE BELONGING HABITS

By now, you've likely identified your top one or two False Belonging Habits. Let's remind ourselves what it's like to live with these habits every day.

Kenta: I believe if I perform well, and I get outside recognition, I will belong.
Are you consistently looking ahead to that next milestone or goal? Is that all you think and talk about, to the point that you tend to have a hard time connecting with people if you're not talking about what you're working on? Even when you do reach that goalpost, do you notice how that long-awaited sense of fulfillment is only temporary?

Underneath it all, do you have this nagging feeling of emptiness?

Amani: I believe if I put others' needs and expectations above my own, I will belong.
Have you unknowingly trained the most important people in your life to believe that you can do everything for everyone and need no

support while doing it? Then, when you *do* need support, do you feel like there's no one you can turn to? Does a sense of loneliness take over in those moments? Do you feel guilty or ashamed asking for help or taking a break?

Mia: I believe if I prevent myself from getting too close, I will be safe emotionally, and then I can belong.
Do you focus on protecting yourself and putting up your guard? When someone close to you is expressing love, do you struggle to accept this love? When you shut someone out, how do you feel after? Alone? Angry? Isolated?

Tate: I believe if I anticipate bad outcomes and try to prevent them, I will prove I'm responsible, and I will belong.
Have you let your anxiety run your life? Do you tend to tense up when your partner calls your name? Do you stress out when sending an email, expecting a blowback? Do you think about it for hours?

As you're in this anxiety loop, do you get glimpses of what this habit is costing you? Do you notice that you're not truly present with those most important to you? Does your anxiety keep you so wound up that you can't seem to relax? Do you experience anxiety hangovers?

Callie: I believe if I repress my emotions, I will belong.
Do you believe you need to monitor your feelings? When you do, does a cycle begin? Your emotions fester, to the point where you *have* to let them out. After you do, you feel intense embarrassment. Next time, you bottle up your emotions and isolate. The pent-up emotions eat away at you until you feel forced to release them again. Does this loop feel familiar to you?

Nolan: I believe if I make the "right" decision, regardless of what I actually think, I will belong.

Has your indecisiveness become a burden to yourself and those around you? Do you find yourself arguing for something when you're not even sure you believe in it? Are you unable to make a decision when you're pressed?

Do you watch people to see what they're thinking and doing in hopes that you can fit in? Do you prioritize what you believe other people want rather than what you want? Do you even know what you want?

Are you tired of feeling frozen? Do you have an aching feeling that you are missing out?

We developed these False Belonging Habits because we thought they'd help us belong. If we do what others want—if we're approved of—then we think we'll belong. But that's not true belonging.

Our Habits are then reinforced by the times when our behavior *does* seem to pay off. Say a new classmate of Mia's invited her to a party. Mia's Habit kicked in and she quickly said no, not wanting to put herself out there. A few weeks later, when the classmate makes a sexist joke, Mia feels a jolt of pride for not letting them in in the first place. She confirms to herself she was right to not get close to THAT person.

In another instance, Nolan couldn't make up his mind about where to go for dinner, so he just let his friend choose. When it ended up being one of the best meals he'd had all year, he was pleased with himself for *not* making up his own mind. He liked the food, and he avoided the stress he feels around making decisions. Seemed like a win-win!

These small wins are how our False Belonging Habits keep us hooked. For a moment, we feel right, and we believe we belong. For a moment. Yet because it was *false* belonging, this warm and fuzzy experience always falls away.

Our Habits also embed fears about what will happen if we *don't* follow these patterns. These fears influence our day-to-day lives far more than we realize. They include:

- A fear of rejection
- A fear of vulnerability
- A fear of our emotions

These fears, just like our False Belonging Habits, are not permanent. They can be addressed and dismantled, and when they are, our Habits cycle is also upended. Let's dive in to see how we can address these fears.

CONFRONTING THE FEARS OF REJECTION AND VULNERABILITY

When we were growing up, our caretakers surely wanted to teach us how to be a functioning part of society. Maybe they pushed us to be the best, like Kenta. Perhaps they praised us for prioritizing taking care of others over ourselves, like Amani. Maybe they led us to second-guess our true opinions in favor of going along with the group consensus, like Nolan. The desire to belong was hardwired in them, just as it is in us, and they were trying their best to help us fit in. Unwittingly, however, they were teaching us that we need to change in some way to belong—that we need to continually work on being better in order to secure our belonging in the tribe.

Now, let's be clear: there's nothing wrong with wanting to improve ourselves. Growth is a necessary part of life, at all stages. The problem lies in believing we'll only belong *when* we're better people, and that we're not worthy of belonging just as we are today.

The message many of us received from school and home and beyond was this: I'm not acceptable just as I am. I have to *do* more and *be* more to earn (and continue to maintain) belonging. From this messaging, we progressively disconnected from our Taho. As our False Belonging Habits formed, we worked increasingly hard to wrangle this elusive sense of belonging.

Over the years, as we form our False Belonging Habits, there is something that humans learned to fear above all else. Something that threatens our fragile sense of belonging—rejection. Being cast out from the tribe. Alone.

Some of us will do just about anything to avoid rejection. We won't go for the job we really want because we think they'll balk at our lack of experience. We'll rewrite a text about rescheduling plans over and over again, trying to find the exact words to relay our thoughts so our friend doesn't take anything we say the wrong way. When we spot an acquaintance in the grocery aisle, we won't go over and say hello, worried they won't remember who we are. When we're in the car with our father-in-law, and he keeps swaying into the next lane, we don't say anything because we don't want to seem rude. Even if our lives are at stake!

There are those of us whose fear of rejection is so deeply buried that we're not even aware of it. We feel pretty confident in our lives, and we don't shirk away from speaking our minds. Yet when we go home and our partner says our name in *that* tone, our nerves go on high alert.

Time and time again, we let our fear of rejection dictate how we act, speak, and live because of the importance of being accepted. It's understandable that we don't want to risk being rejected.

So, yes, we understand why we currently operate this way, but what are the consequences of trying so hard to avoid rejection?

We end up learning to fear vulnerability.

If we're vulnerable, we're, by definition, unmasking our innermost emotions and thoughts. Even though vulnerability is the ticket to intimacy and connection, in our minds, the more we expose ourselves, the more brutally we can be rejected.

We may have learned that crying is pitiful. Anger is unattractive and inappropriate. Fear is weakness. Some even learned that sharing these feelings with others is something you just didn't do; you sucked it up and soldiered on. Doing what's expected of us—having it all together—*that's* how we belong.

However, think of what happens when we do this. Say we hide our truth and put up a front, and then someone responds positively to us. In this instance, we might think that hiding our vulnerability led to us belonging. Except *we* are not really belonging at times like this; the persona that we've created is.

Think about it like this: would you rather have a friend who only likes you based on the "front" you present, or a friend who knows the depth of who you are and still enjoys your presence?

Would you rather shrug off an insecurity you're feeling, or speak about it with your partner in an open way?

Would you rather live under immense pressure from your parents' expectations of you, or speak your truth to them and finally release yourself from the tension?

The choice might seem obvious, but just because we can see the power of vulnerability doesn't mean the fear immediately goes away.

These aversions to vulnerability and rejection are deeply ingrained in us. In fact, we are so conditioned to avoid rejection that this fear exists at the *body level*; research has shown that our brain subconsciously interprets potential rejection in the same way it views physical threats. Think about when you've been asked to do something you were afraid of—perhaps giving a speech in public. Did your heart race? Were you sweaty and clammy? These moments can incite the same level of arousal as coming across a bear on a trail. Our bodies and our psyches want to survive, and it seems we've bundled all types of threats into one big pile of fearful responses that causes us to ask, "Will I be okay? Will I be safe? Will I survive this?"

Yet, when we're going to give a speech, *physically* we are safe. So, what is it that feels threatened? What feels in danger?

Our belonging. Our worth. Our lovability. Our Taho.

CALL ON YOUR COURAGE

Our Taho is our very foundation; it's our connection with our true selves, with those we love, and with nature. Our Taho is our deepest innate source of confidence and stability, like the roots of a tree.

If we ignore or deny our Taho, we can become a shadow of who we could be. We might lose sight of our passions, our sense of purpose, and most painfully, our joy. It can even get to the point where we fall under the illusion that we no longer have innate value and love, and we experience a kind of emotional collapse—where we coast on autopilot.

Disconnection is illusionary—we cannot truly be disconnected from our Taho, but the belief we are is profoundly painful and debilitating. Have you ever reached this point in your own life? Wouldn't you do just about anything to avoid experiencing it again?

That's what we're fighting for: the opportunity to fully claim our belonging, embrace our Taho, and share this belonging with everyone.

But how do we do this when we're in such pain? As contrary as it may sound, the doorway to our Taho is our wounding. Does it sound a little scary? Vulnerability is like that. It hurts for a minute, and then it becomes our freedom.

In tough moments, we need some extra help to push through insecurities, judgments, or conditioned thoughts that are trying to pull us back toward our False Belonging Habits.

Thankfully, we have built-in tools that we've developed throughout our lives, qualities that are always ready and able to help us conquer our fears of rejection and vulnerability. A tool you already own is courage.

Some people might think of courage as something reserved for firefighters, skydivers, or explorers. For people who do big, impressive feats most wouldn't even dare attempt. But is that really true?

Think of a time when you were scared to say something to an important person in your life, but you said it anyway. Can you connect with that feeling you had in your gut when you finally spoke your truth? Yes, scared, but what else?

Courage. *That* was courage.

Despite the fear, you pushed through anyway. Regardless of the result—you were brave in that moment. Our lives are a collection of fierce moments like this, moments when we were terrified or nervous but did the thing anyway.

This isn't to say we were fearless every single day. Maybe some days you didn't push through the fear. But if you're old enough to read this book, you've made it through thousands of new and scary situations. You've felt afraid, in thousands of ways, throughout your life. Still, you forged ahead anyway.

That takes courage.

You've built up your bravery day after day, week after week, year after year. If you had no courage, you'd be long dead.

So, let's take a moment to acknowledge all those forgotten days when you faced what scared you. When you didn't hide or run away. When you simply got out of bed. It's time to update the truth about yourself.

Have you been courageous? YES!

Can you be courageous again? YES!

Are you courageous? YES!

Feel that. Take it in. Take a deep breath and let yourself experience this truth.

YES! I am courageous!

While it's often been overshadowed by our False Belonging Habits, courage is available to tap into at any time. It helps to take an inventory of moments from our lives when our courage shone through. It's incredibly powerful to write out these experiences so they're easy to refer back to—and embody—when we lose our balance.

First, think about a specific experience where you were courageous; for example, getting back into dating after a breakup. Next, write down all the courageous actions you took: filling out an authentic profile on a dating app, pushing through the fear of not meeting the right person, connecting with someone new and opening your heart up again. Finally, rewrite these actions to anchor them as truths about yourself:

- Am I the person who decided to be authentic? YES!
- Am I the person who continued to face potential rejection on new dates? YES
- Am I the person who took a risk to love again? YES

Write down as many of these experiences as you can to create a courage inventory. Think of some of the most challenging times in your life in which you demonstrated courage—great triumphs that you can remember viscerally in your whole being.

The best way to create this anchor is to visualize the moment. What did the room look like? Was your heart racing? What was the other person wearing? Was there music playing in the background? Traffic driving by? Become connected—visually, viscerally, and emotionally—to these experiences from your inventory. Then, when you need to call upon your courage, these vivid experiences will be at the front of your mind. You'll be able to connect back to this evidence from your life, reminding your body and mind that you are, in fact, courageous.

When we get to the point where our body can feel the truth of our courage, it's much more difficult for our False Belonging Habits to sway us into believing otherwise.

ACKNOWLEDGE YOUR RESILIENCE

This courage, this ability to face our fears, is profound and builds our strength and character. There's another quality that is equally as powerful: resilience.

It takes courage to continue to push through our wounding, and there is where we find our resilience. And that is a quality we already possess, forged through our experiences. For one person, their resilience came from having to face their mom's anxiety every day after school. Someone else could have built up a resilient nature from having to take care of their little brother while their parents worked. Many of us have gone through a harrowing experience, but then put our heads down and only focused on "just getting through it," ignoring the tenacity it took to do so.

This resilience is what will keep us going as we learn to break the cycle we've been stuck in. We've been following our False Belonging Habits for a very long time. There will always be moments when we lose our way for a bit. And that's okay! Falling down is part of the learning process. What matters is that after we fall, we can choose to pick ourselves back up and try again—something we have already done thousands of times. That's resilience.

In addition to helping us keep moving forward, our resilience aids in the development of new abilities. When we slammed on the brake too hard during our first solo drive, we built more awareness about gently easing into a stop next time.

When we mismanaged our time and were late to a meeting, we recalibrated to get organized and be timelier.

When we let a bully's hurtful words tear us down, we showed resilience by continuing to live our life, despite what anyone else had to say.

Sometimes it's easier to see these changes within the context of big life challenges. Have you ever been let go from a job? Have you filed for bankruptcy? Have you been hospitalized for an illness or injury? Have you brought up a really difficult subject to someone? What deeper awareness or skill did you gain out of it?

What if we changed the way we looked at failure in our day-to-day lives? What if we looked at failure through the lens of an appreciation for our resilience? For example, after a breakup, you learned that you *can* live without that other person. You were able to push through the pain and emerge on the other side. You went on to create new friendships and relationships. That is a fact to be celebrated! That's resilience.

Let's take a moment to reflect and notice the resilience in our own lives. Take a calm, deep breath. Slow everything down for a moment. Think back on a time when you've failed. Notice the painful memories. Allow yourself to feel them. Once you've given the emotional memories their due attention, think about the weeks and months after these events.

Did you let this failure drag you down forever? Did you eventually get back up? What ability do you have now that you didn't have before this failure?

This is you, tapping into your resilience. Imagine if you reframed your life with this perspective of perseverance and resilience.

Are you the person who got back up, time and time again? YES!

Are you the person who has developed extraordinary skills and gifts *because* you failed? YES!

Have you lived through hard things? YES! And will you continue to push through each hurdle that comes your way? YES!

Are you resilient?

YES, I am resilient!

So often, we have a tough time recognizing resilience in ourselves. To experience your own resilience, take some time to create a resilience inventory, just like you did with your courage.

Think about a specific experience that you found challenging; for example, losing your job. Next, write down all the ways in which you were resilient: giving yourself time to process the news, investigating a broader scope of employment and trying on new options, having faith in yourself, getting a new job and dedicating yourself to it. Finally, rewrite these actions to anchor them as truths about yourself:

- Am I the person who accepted my situation? YES
- Am I the person who continued to apply to jobs, no matter how beaten down I felt? YES
- Am I the person that didn't let this setback crush my dreams? The person who still pursued what I wanted to do? YES

Allow yourself to suspend any self-judgment you hold about each situation so you can see what you actually gained from that event. Just like you did with your courage inventory, allow the factual evidence of your own resilience to present itself to you by recreating these challenging moments. When you can fully see and acknowledge how you factually picked yourself back up, your mind cannot dismiss the reality of your resilience so easily. The body remembers the actual moment when you overcame what initially seemed impossible. This memory lives in our very cells. That's resilience.

The Crew members repeatedly dug into their own courage and resilience when they began to shift into a life of *Avive la Vie*. For example, it took a lot of courage for Amani to sit still in her discomfort and accept the food and service from Rowan, Mia, and Kenta at The Hearth. Nolan tapped into his resilience after his breakup with Tori and painful injury. He didn't let his mistake define him; he picked himself back up and got on with his life.

Can you recognize these truths?

Your experiences of resilience and courage are no small thing! They are tangible pieces of evidence of your enduring strength. Despite all the hardships, adversity, oppression, and even tragedy you've faced, you are a courageous and resilient human being.

This is who you are.

Embrace the resilience and courage you've built up throughout your life. You can harness this power to help you find your way out of false belonging and into embracing your inner wholeness. This starts by walking through the Three Doors.

MOVING PAST YOUR REACTIONS

Every day, we find ourselves faced with challenges. Maybe you find a nail in your tire before driving to work. Maybe your daughter doesn't want to go to her dentist appointment. Maybe you're worried about something your spouse said. In these moments, we often get caught up in our mind's narrative. "I shouldn't have to deal with this." "Why won't she just listen to me?" "What did he mean by that?"

As we follow this train of thought, driven by our False Belonging Habits, uncomfortable emotions start popping up. If we're focusing on the inconvenience of having to get our tire patched, we might blame the tire for our emotional reaction. If we're thinking of how our daughter is going to have a meltdown and not get a thorough dental cleaning, we might become anxious or focus our blame on our daughter.

In reality, these stories aren't the real issues that need our attention. The real source of our pain, disillusionment, and lack of belonging is hidden underneath all that chatter and reactivity.

This is one of the realizations that can be toughest to wrap our minds around, because we've been so conditioned to believe that the problem is *out there somewhere*. When Kenta was beating himself up for not winning the proposal at the architectural firm, he was sure that the problem was that the clients liked Becca better. However, the actual cause of his distress wasn't the clients, or even Becca; his own sense of self-worth was coming into question.

The same is true when your daughter throws a fit about going to the dentist. Under all those seemingly good reasons for your aggravation lies the truth. You may be questioning if you're a good enough parent, if your impatience with her means something deeper about you, which leads to questioning your innate value.

Even a nail in your tire isn't the true source of your frustration or worry. You might find that you're telling yourself the story that you screwed up somehow, or that you'll be late to work and it will reflect poorly on you. It might even become "I'm not good enough!"

Every day, we go chasing after love and value *outside* of ourselves. We believe if we give enough, prepare enough, follow expectations enough, then we'll belong. The alternative, where we embrace our innate worth, is so much less stressful. Our Taho is our true home—the place in us where we know our worth and our true essence.

The way to begin repairing the connection to our Taho is through the Three Doors.

Imagine that our beautiful essence of innate love and value—our Taho—exists as a glowing ball of pure life force within our core. Every moment of our lives, this inherent power is within us, steady and constant, unable to be dimmed or lost.

This light is the most comforting, warm illumination you've ever experienced. Think of it like the night-light that kept you safe from the monsters as a child, or the heat lamp that offers rays of warmth on a cold winter day. When you truly focus on the light, you feel nurtured, soothed, and uplifted.

Imagine that this pure essence is a ball of electricity that has a single outlet, with one cord plugged into it that runs throughout your entire body. When this cord is properly connected, you're fully tapped into the energy of your innate wholeness—your value and love. You feel empowered, confident, and charged. You feel safe, connected, and grounded.

195

Though we're always plugged into our innate essence, the strength of our connection can vary. When we focus primarily on outer stress and blame, we can lose conscious touch with our inner life force and experience a sense of "low voltage," leaving us feeling depleted, lost, and alone. We may even question if we are loveable, if we are valuable, or if there is hope for us.

To see what happens when we dip into this poor-connection mode, let's return to the example of your daughter throwing a tantrum about going to the dentist. In distressing situations, we've been taught by our conditioned mindset to react quickly—to take control of the situation and fix the problem. As soon as you see her quivering lip and tear-stained cheeks, you reactively try to *think* your way to a solution. *If we're late to the dentist, they might not be able to see her at all today. Then I'll have to reschedule and take ANOTHER morning off. And who knows when they'll even be able to reschedule her. Why can't she just behave?!*

There's often one overarching theme to these thoughts: "I don't want this!"

I don't want my daughter to defy me. I don't want to be at odds with her.

I don't want to have to reschedule the dentist appointment.

I don't want to have to talk to my boss about taking another morning off work.

As soon as we dive into this frenzy of thoughts, our "voltage" can drop and our connection to our Taho seems to disappear. We're focusing on external factors—and we're (unknowingly) letting these other people and situations appear to determine our innate value and love. It feels familiar to react in this way— even comfortable, because it's *typical* for us to react, and even react about reacting. It feels familiar. We feel in control for a moment.

This reactivity may well be our default process, but we can learn to instead stop, consciously breathe, and reconnect with our Taho.

This is the gift of noticing moments of "low voltage." This awareness has the potential to be our wake-up call—our chance to observe the feelings and thoughts that led to us questioning our innate love and value. A low voltage moment is a powerful opportunity to *choose connection*.

What do you choose?

CHAPTER 11

OPENING THE THREE DOORS

S ay we spot a moment of low voltage—a time when we are feel-ing out of control and afraid of what others will think of us. In that moment, we're presented with an opportunity to reconnect with our Taho. How do we go about restoring that connection? Let's walk through the Three Doors.

This transformation starts by first realizing just how vital con-nection really is for our happiness, our well-being, our mental health, everything! All of us share a deep desire to belong, and we can work toward making that connection a priority in our lives—not just with the people around us, but also within our-selves. No matter what situation we are faced with, connection comes first.

When we're about to move into disconnection (which hap-pens much more frequently than many of us realize), we can walk through the Three Doors to return to an authentic connection—starting with our own inner sense of belonging. The more we utilize these doors, the more natural it will become to prioritize connection throughout our lives.

Each of the Three Doors has a unique purpose. Door One focuses on not following the train of thought that leads us to react. Instead, we pause. We're slowing everything down so we can take the time to connect.

Door Two prioritizes the connection to our emotional body. We're letting go of any agenda or story so we can be present with our discomfort, attuning to our feelings.

Door Three allows us to re-establish the connection between our mind and emotional body. Using the intelligence of our emotional body, we remind ourselves that our innate love and value are alive and well, regardless of what is happening in the moment.

Let's see what it looks like to walk through the Three Doors, reconnect with ourselves, and restore a sense of belonging.

DOOR ONE: PAUSING YOUR CONDITIONED THOUGHTS

The first indicator that we're about to lose connection is when we're being reactive. When faced with a difficult situation, we often re-spond with a knee-jerk reaction such as defending ourselves, blam-ing the other person, or withdrawing altogether. These reactions can quickly sever any connection we were experiencing—with the other person and with ourselves. To prioritize connection, we can learn to pause the thoughts that lead to these reactions before we do any damage.

To see what this looks like in real time, let's go to Tate. He's recently moved back into his home and is soaking up living with Molly and his daughters again. This is fairly early in Tate's journey to living from a connection-based mindset; he's familiar with the Three Doors, but this is one of the first times he has implemented it in his own life.

One day, Tate's reading a book at the kitchen table when Molly comes home from lunch with a friend. As soon as she walks in, Tate can tell Molly is excited about something.

"Cheryl got an electric car! And she absolutely loves it!" Molly starts listing off all the features of her friend's car. Then Molly adds, "We should really look into getting one, you know. I think it could be a really good fit for us! There are bigger models, too, so we can put all the..."

Tate doesn't hear the rest of Molly's sentence. Immediately, he's pulled into his conditioned thinking. *She doesn't want to get one now, does she? We just fixed the roof—we don't have the money for that kind of purchase! How can she be so careless about our finances?*

He's about to respond with, "You're not being serious, right? We can't afford that right now." But before Tate opens his mouth, he recognizes that *certain tone* his thoughts have. Tate is familiar with that tone (as most of us are), so this acts as his signal that he's listening to his conditioned thoughts. Instead of reacting, he takes a deep breath, and then another.

This is the vital first step of Door One. In order to respond in a different way, we have to hit pause. Pause on our narrative. Pause on reacting and saying something we'll later regret. Pause on continuing the conversation. Pause on everything.

While it may seem easy to pause like this, it's often not. Most of us have relied on our knee-jerk reactions our whole lives. We have this immense urge to point out why this sucks or why the other person isn't being fair or why this shouldn't be happening. And since that initial impulse can be so strong, we have to physically stop ourselves from saying those things by taking a deep breath.

The benefit of deep breathing is twofold. Not only does it stop our lips from moving, it also helps us to pump the brakes on our False Belonging Habits. A full breath allows us to pause the story long enough to become *aware* of the thoughts that are swirling around, rather than automatically following them. We're becoming the witness of our reactivity instead of engaging in it.

In this pause, Tate observes his tone and intended reaction of: "You're not being serious, right?" As he does, Tate sees the scene play out in his head of what would happen if he *had* made this comment.

In his mind's eye, Molly comes back with, "Are *you* serious? You're shutting me down before we can even have a conversation."

"I didn't shut you down," Tate would say. "It's just unrealistic, so I wanted to make sure you weren't thinking it was."

Then Molly's voice would rise. "And what if I was? When do we get to enjoy this money we work so damn hard for, Tate? And why do you always get the final say about what we can and can't afford?"

"You think *I* always get the final say? With all you buy?" Tate would argue, raising his voice to match hers.

Tate *knows* this is what will happen because he's gone through this debate five hundred times before, and he feels every sensation as if he's having the debate again now. He can feel his frustration about to boil over. He senses that tension building in his muscles. He fully experiences the weight of his anxiety as it spreads throughout every limb.

Right now, Tate is in the storm. He's having a visceral experience of the hurricane that awaits him if he reacts to his wife. And *this* is his motivator to respond in a different way.

Few of us are aware of the connection/disconnection that happens in a heated moment like this because we're singularly focused on saying our piece. But when we can actually picture—and experience—the disconnection that is about to transpire, we experience the proof of how this old reactive approach has not worked in the past.

This is the power of Door One. It makes our choice clear. Instead of repeating the same argument, we need to prioritize the connection.

With this awareness, Tate has convinced himself not to react to Molly. This internal chaos was his signal to stop focusing on his story about Molly and shift to looking inward about what's going on for *him*. So, he says, "Honey, I'm gonna take a minute before we talk about this more." Molly, unbothered, nods and goes to check in on the girls.

In this example, Tate recognizes his old patterns of reactive thinking. We often recognize these thoughts because they sound a certain way, that old tone, and they serve as a sign that we need to pause before we react.

The more familiar you become with your low voltage periods, the easier it becomes to notice them. Before long, hearing that certain tone in your thoughts takes on a similar nature as recognizing that you're hungry. When you feel that emptiness in your stomach, you're not *actively* thinking about the fact that you're hungry. You just feel the sensation in your belly, and you know what it means. That's the goal—to simply feel a sensation and know you need to walk through the Three Doors.

While Tate has managed his reaction, he now needs to address his feelings. Let's see how Tate navigates his emotions as he moves through Door Two.

DOOR TWO: ATTUNING TO YOUR EMOTIONAL BODY

After being mentored by the Crew, Tate knows he needs to harness his courage to fully experience his emotions. He decides to head out to the backyard to find a quiet space to do this. As he paces around the patio table, he lets those judgmental thoughts about Molly flow back into his mind. *Is she serious? We just bought a new roof! My god, she's being so irresponsible.*

As Tate replays these thoughts, he is mindful not to get sucked into the narrative. Instead, he focuses on the feeling that accompanies these judgments: irritation. He allows himself to fully sink into the frustration, reminding himself that this irritation is valid. *You're pissed off. That's okay. You're allowed to be pissed off.*

As the feeling of anger intensifies, Tate knows that he's descended into his emotional body. Now, he changes gears—he turns the judgmental thoughts toward himself. *Are you serious, Tate? You're going to let her convince you to buy a new car you don't need? You're more irresponsible than she is!*

Almost instantly, the irritation shifts into sharp anxiety. Tate shifts his attention away from those condescending thoughts and now puts his whole focus on experiencing the nuances of the emotions within his body. He feels the dread of not having "enough"; the panic of not being able to provide for his family; the distress of being irresponsible.

Tate gasps, suddenly desperate for air. But he still feels the heaviness of this burden of anxiety, dragging him down further. *You're okay, Tate. You're anxious. Your emotions matter. You've got this,* he tells himself, pushing through the suffocating feeling to take a deep breath. As he does, he hears Rowan's voice in his head: "Your anxiety sure is costing you a lot."

The cost. Tate sinks down into a patio chair. The anxiety isn't so acute anymore, replaced by a deep sense of grief. Tate knows full well what his anxiety has cost him. In this moment, he re-experiences the weight of all those consequences. Watching his daughters drive away with Molly. Eating pizza alone in his truck, feeling hopeless and helpless.

His family is just behind the kitchen door, yet Tate has never felt so alone.

He leans forward slightly, looking at a crack in the concrete. Tears start falling as the overwhelming loneliness takes over, and soon he is sobbing. All Tate can feel is how much his anxiety has taken from him. How he can't even enjoy a simple moment of joy with his wife without jumping to overthinking. The anguish seems all-encompassing.

With his head in his hands, Tate grieves what he nearly lost. There's so much he could have done differently. He fully gives himself to his emotions, not trying to control anything as his chest heaves.

After a few minutes, Tate is able to take a wheezy breath, then a full one. Soon, his body feels loose and relaxed. His heartbeat returns to a normal pace. His breath slows. As he looks out at the trees swaying in the breeze, he feels a sense of calm.

The heavy anxiety is dissipating. The grief is lifting. Tate has attuned to his emotions, and he is now finding a sense of peace and acceptance.

After hearing Molly talk about getting a new car, Tate's mind started running with a story about how careless she was. This is what most of us do: stay focused on the judgmental narrative about the other person or situation and react from that perspective. Yet underneath this story is something most of us ignore—something vital to walking through the Three Doors.

Our emotions.

This is what Tate tapped into in Door Two. He used the story he was making up about Molly to descend into the initial emotion he was feeling. In his case, that emotion was frustration; you may experience something different. No matter what emotion shows up for you first—irritation, disappointment, fear, shame—that feeling is almost always tied to the story you're making up about the situation or the other person.

Tate paused before he reacted so he could distance himself from his story long enough to tap into—and welcome—the emotion that was coming up. Once he attuned to this initial feeling, he knew he had to go deeper to get to the real source of his discomfort. The Crew had taught him that the easiest way to do this was by flipping the judgment he was having about the other person back on himself.

Tate could do this because he was *aware* he was highly reactive. He knew his judgments about Molly weren't founded in truth but were instead a defense mechanism orchestrated by his False Belonging Habit. We were trained to believe that the problem is *out there*, remember?

When we flip the script and judge ourselves, we move past the initial emotion and reach something else: our underlying anxiety. In this anxiety, we can see that we were merely projecting our fears and insecurities onto the other person or the situation. This anxiety isn't about anything or anyone else; it's about *us*. In order to move through Door Two, we make space for our anxiety.

However, it's not always easy to dive into our anxiety headfirst. In fact, you may have read the story above and thought, *I don't want to do that! Why would I put myself through something like this?* This is because many of us have been taught to disconnect from the feelings, sensations, and emotions that pop into our awareness so that we can fit within society's expectations. As a result, we didn't learn to feel safe welcoming the intuitive, emotional place within us—what we call our emotional body. Instead, we stuff down our emotions and let them fester within us, and that's where they'll stay until we do something to release them.

Our emotional body carries enormous wisdom that will help us embrace connection, but we can't *think* our way to those insights. To access this information, we have to surrender to the anxiety and emotional pain we've ignored for so long. We have to go through the discomfort—and come out the other side. And while that process seems intimidating at first, this emotional release is a good thing, and it's never as bad or as scary as you may think it will be.

Also, keep in mind that every attunement session isn't going to look the same. In this example, Tate was dealing with one of his biggest stressors: his fear of not being responsible with his finances. When you're faced with your foundational fears, you're more likely to have big emotions and a great deal of discomfort. As you become more familiar with attuning to your emotional body, these feelings of intensity and unease will lessen.

When we allow ourselves to be vulnerable and experience the truth of who we are, we unlock a new level of empathy toward ourselves and others. Think about it like this: right now, do you feel more empathetic to Tate than when we first met him, or less?

The reason we feel more compassion toward Tate is that he's finally accessing his truth. He's not trying to excuse his behavior or "fix" his habits; he's simply accepting what he's done, what it's cost him, and who he is without trying to change anything. Just as you likely feel more connected to Tate, you'll likely feel more empathetic toward yourself at the end of Door Two.

While you may not be familiar with this process of sitting with your emotions, you have likely seen the benefits of this type of emotional release. Can you think of the last time you had a long cry after an emotional event, such as losing a loved one? Can you remember how your body felt looser? How even though the grief was still there, you felt a sense of relief? In that moment, you reached a similar place to what Tate experienced. And the beautiful thing is that this feeling of relief isn't reserved only for those extreme moments in life. This is what the Crew learned from Rowan: that attuning on an ongoing basis is what allows a true transformation of our sense of belonging.

The ability to honor your emotions is a beautiful invitation to give yourself. Now, your feelings are free to be accessed—and appreciated—any time.

After attuning to his emotional body, the heavy lifting is done. Tate is at the doorstep of Door Three, and he has just one thing left to do before walking through it.

DOOR THREE: AFFIRMING YOUR TAHO

Now that his internal storm has passed, Tate is noticing what remains: his love for his daughters, his appreciation for his wife, and his gratitude for their lives together. As intense as the anxiety and grief were, they were nothing compared to the potency of the love radiating from Tate's heart in this moment.

In this peaceful space, Tate remembers that this is when the Crew asks themselves a question: "Where is my sense of love and value?"

So, he slowly breathes out and asks himself, *Where is my sense of love and value?*

He doesn't even need to think about it. *It's right here.*

He follows up with, *Does buying a car or not buying a car change my love and value?*

Tate chuckles at the ridiculousness of the question. He can feel how his Taho is alive and thriving within him, and that there's nothing he could do to lose it. Now that he's brought himself to a place of connection, he knows that he can have a productive conversation with his wife—one that can bring them together instead of driving them apart.

Door Three is a more subtle step than the other two. You're asking yourself a question, "Where is my sense of love and value?" But you already know the answer—your body is simply reminding your mind what it is. Like Tate, you are reaffirming that your Taho is in you, not *out there*, and that no one and nothing can take it away from you.

While it may seem like Tate's realization about his love and value came from his mind, that isn't the case. Attuning to his emotional body is what allowed Tate to realign with his Taho. This is because our Taho lives within our emotional body. Our innate value and love exist as experiences within our body rather than as analytical concepts. This means when we're in a reactive state, the only way we're able to access our Taho is by sitting with our uncomfortable emotions and attuning to our emotional body.

Going through the Three Doors is profound because we're able to feel how our False Belonging Habits, though they've tried to help us, have actually led to us feeling anxious and disconnected. By pressing pause, sitting in our pain, and accepting all our emotions, we're able to experience how our innate love and value are, in fact, still intact, and have always been safe.

CHAPTER 12

KEEPING YOUR MIND IN CHECK

When you walk through the Three Doors for the first time, you might find that your mind wants to hurry the process along to figure out the source of your discomfort and get it over with. As much as our minds desperately want to skip straight to the end, we *must* walk through all Three Doors. We have to pause and allow ourselves to attune to our emotional body. If you don't, then this process will just be an interesting thought experiment.

For instance, imagine if we had gone up to Tate after he'd first talked with Molly and asked, "Hey Tate, does your innate value depend on whether Molly gets a new car?" His response would have been, "What? Of course not." Tate would have been able to see that, logically, his love and value didn't have anything to do with whether Molly got a new car. Regardless, his body would have still believed that it did. Without going through the Three Doors, Tate likely would have reacted and gotten into an argument with Molly—even after being asked this question.

We've often defaulted to our mind as being the ultimate system of intelligence. But with the Three Doors, we instead shift to trusting the wisdom of the emotional body.

To get a clearer picture of how we do this, let's look at a few more examples of how we can create a balance of our mind and emotional body during the Three Doors. Say you find out you didn't get a job you interviewed for. When subscribing to your False Belonging Habits, your conditioned thoughts will start racing, blaming the employer or yourself. *They could have asked better questions. I should have been more prepared.*

If you pause this train of thought and attune to your emotional body, you'll be able to return to a centered state of being. Only then, after your body has convinced your mind that you're okay, can you ask yourself, *Do I still have innate love and value after not getting this job? Did I lose it?* Now you can not only *think* how absurd that question is, but you can also feel in your bones how getting or not getting a job could never define you.

Many of us will experience a pushback within ourselves right about now: "There's no way I'm really attaching my sense of worth and love to something as trivial as not getting one job." That would be our conditioned thoughts piping up yet again. We don't want to believe that this is true because we've been conditioned to believe that the world around us is what's causing our distress. But it *is* true, and the more we practice walking through the Doors, the more we can recognize it.

Let's look at another example: your partner says you work too much. Again, your mind may go to defensive mode. *I'm giving my all to provide for us!* But, after pausing this narrative and attuning to our emotional body, we can then ask ourselves, *Can overworking ever make me not lovable or not valuable at a core level?* Again, we're able to comprehend analytically and experience physically how working could never relate to our inner value or love.

Let's look at one more example. Say you've gained some weight. You can imagine how vicious the thoughts can be. *I look terrible. Everyone is going to notice.* Isn't it heartbreaking how something as inconsequential as an expanding body can alter how valuable we think we are? Yet this is the illusion so many of us are trapped under. This is why we can so easily lose sight of our Taho.

The good news is that it's just that—an illusion. Put a pause on these thoughts and attune to your emotional body. After those self-criticizing thoughts have faded, ask yourself, *Am I still valuable and lovable now that I gained weight?*

Or course I am. And I always will be.

Each and every one of us, regardless of what we say, do, think, or look like, is valuable and worthy of love. It's not an opinion; it's the core truth. We are inherently valuable. We are always lovable. Every one of us has courage and resilience. When we pause, attune, and reconnect with our Taho, we can experience how we are beautiful and powerful beyond measure.

TRUST THE EMOTIONAL BODY

Once we have our mind in check, it takes guts to trust our emotional body. We have so much working against us: our fear of rejection, unfamiliarity with our emotions and anxiety, and our False Belonging Habits. But working through this anxiety is what allows us to finally reconnect with our innate love and value. It's the way *in*.

Think of your commitment to walking through the Three Doors like taking an ice bath. When you first step in, every inch of your skin stings. Your mind, unfamiliar with the pain, is screaming, "Get out! Get out!" But you know the benefits, so you push through the prickly discomfort. Soon, the sting fades and a warmth seems to surround your body as you acclimate. You can now sit in ease, soaking up the benefits of pushing through the pain.

We go through a similar experience when we reconnect with our Taho; we have to embrace our emotional distress to reach our innate value and love. Allowing ourselves to be with this tension is one of the most empowering choices we can make. We're taking a stand against mindlessly following the part we think we have to play in this world. We're telling ourselves, "I deserve to have a say in my belonging."

In these moments when staying with our emotional pain feels shaky, we can call on our courage. We know we can do hard things. We have done so many hard things. Our courage inventory is full of evidence of courageous things we've actually done. Even when it's overwhelmingly uncomfortable, we *can* push through our fear and anxiety to reconnect with our inner essence. We can channel Rowan. This is what he did with the Crew, right? Encouraged and championed them as they sat in their emotional distress?

Be your own Rowan. In these difficult moments, remind yourself, "I got this."

So, let's repeat this one more time, because our minds can have such a hard time accepting this: in times of high reactivity, attuning to your emotional body, welcoming every experience of your being without attempting to control anything, is what allows you to feel connected with your Taho.

Attuning, and the Three Doors as a whole, is a practice of trust. You're surrendering yourself to the process, accepting whatever outcome transpires. Some sessions will be more intense, others less so. And the more we attune, the more fluid we become with this process. As we build the muscle of pausing, attuning, and reconnecting to our innate value and love, it becomes easier and more intuitive. Just as feeding your hunger is vital to your health, walking through the Three Doors becomes vital to maintaining your sense of connection and belonging.

CHAPTER 13

THRIVING THROUGH AUTHENTIC COMMUNICATION

After we've solidified our relationship with our Taho through the Three Doors, we can experience what it means to fully belong with ourselves. We're letting go of attempting to belong through inauthentic ways. We're building up our muscle of self-acceptance, and we can feel at peace with who we are—and man, does it feel good!

If we each spent our lives in our own bubble, we could stop here. We could simply soak up this sense of self-belonging and thrive.

But we don't live in isolation. Remember, we're wired for connection. We're driven at a primal level to seek out friendships and partnerships. We're empathetic creatures who experience our most profound levels of bliss and purpose when we authentically engage with other people.

This is why Rowan lives as he does. His mother taught him that while he can create a utopia within his own mind, he'll be most fulfilled when he's part of a community of people he can be fully open and vulnerable with. He keeps creating opportunities for connection, from when he asked Amani to be The Hearth's taste tester to when he invited Tate to yoga and asked Callie to join in on the Crew's hike. In every situation, Rowan created a space where those around him could be completely transparent, authentic, and fully themselves. We can create similar experiences of community and connection in our own lives through Authentic Communication.

Think of Authentic Communication as sharing your experience of walking through the Three Doors. When we learn how to communicate in this way, a whole new depth of connection will become available. We experience a new degree of joy from strengthening the bonds with those we most care about. We discover that actually *vocalizing* our honest thoughts creates a visceral experience in our emotional body, which can lead to long-term change; a change that can help us emulate Rowan. Let's dive into how you can integrate this change into your own life, starting with an example from Nolan's life.

Nolan is at a cookout in his parents' backyard, celebrating his mom's birthday. He's laughing at his dad's joke when his uncle walks through the gate. "Happy Birthday!" he yells, greeting Nolan's mom.

Nolan slowly backs away from the group, seeking reprieve under the red maple's shade. He pulls out his phone, hoping it'll be enough to dissuade his uncle from coming over.

It isn't.

His uncle beelines over to Nolan. "There he is! My future accountant!" he says, throwing his arm around Nolan's shoulder.

Nolan laughs uncomfortably. "Uncle Leo, I said I'd think about the job. I haven't said 'yes' yet."

His uncle smiles. "But talk about good timing, huh? My accountant leaves right when you need a job. Couldn't have planned it better myself!"

Nolan swallows hard. A few months ago, he had worked up the nerve to leave his accounting job to try and pursue his true passion: archaeology. He'd been talking with a volunteer organization in South America, and he found out he might be able to snag a spot volunteering at a research site. However, his savings were dwindling, and the accounting job at his uncle's painting business would help with those impending bills.

Nolan's thoughts sound off. *Look how excited he is to be able to offer me this job. He's always been there for me. What am I thinking anyway, running off to the jungle? I'm just going to eat through my savings with nothing to show for it.*

Just before Nolan is about to say, "You know what? Yeah, I'll take you up on it," he recognizes that *certain tone* his thoughts have. He's been utilizing the Three Doors for a little while now, so he knows it's time to walk through them. He can see how his False Belonging Habit is flaring up, and this is his signal to hit pause and begin Door One.

As he pauses, Nolan can imagine how the scenario could play out if he accepted the job just to make ends meet and make his uncle happy. "Wonderful!" Leo would cheer, raising Nolan's hand in the air. "Guess who's officially part of the Russo Paint team?" he'd announce to the family.

As the rest of his family members would come over and congratulate Nolan, he'd have a sinking feeling in his gut that he'd attempt to hide with a smile. That heaviness would only grow as the reality of what Nolan had just given up would sink in.

So, rather than revert back to his habit of going along and agreeing, Nolan pivots. "I'm gonna grab some water. Want anything?" Nolan asks his uncle.

"A root beer would be great. Thanks." As Nolan walks inside, he takes this as his opportunity to walk through Door Two and attune to his emotional body.

Nolan heads to the bathroom, where he leans against the vanity. He knows he needs to descend into his emotions, so he lets the judgmental thoughts about the conversation flow into his mind. *Uncle Leo knows better than me. Everyone knows better than me.*

The sadness that accompanies these ideas is swift. Nolan welcomes the melancholy, reminding himself, *You can be sad right now. Your sadness is valid. Your emotions matter.*

Once he's fully immersed in the sadness, Nolan turns the judgments toward himself. *What kind of a person lets others think, feel, and decide for them? I'm pathetic. I'm useless. How can I ever trust myself?*

With each statement, Nolan feels the disappointment disappear as a sense of anxiety fills its space. Knowing he's now fully experiencing his emotional body, Nolan finds the courage to welcome all the aspects of anxiety he's experiencing. There's the fear of making the wrong decision. The apprehension of trying something new. The tension from potentially letting down someone he loves. His False Belonging Habit of self-doubt is showing its face. His heart rate soars, and a flush of heat spreads throughout his body. Nolan breathes through these uncomfortable feelings, telling himself, *My experience matters. I'm okay. This anxiety is okay. I'm doubting myself again. Stay with this feeling.*

The realization that his self-doubt is acting up is like a stab to the gut. Nolan can feel just how much his self-doubt has cost him throughout his life. Nolan lets his head fall as the pangs of regret swoop in sharp and fast. The years he'd wasted pursuing a career that he wasn't even enthusiastic about. The wedge that he'd driven between his parents and himself when they were trying their best to help him. The end of his relationship with Tori.

Once again, his thoughts drift to that night in his apartment when Tori said, "I'm done talking." The pain is not as overwhelming as it once was, but Nolan's eyes still brim with tears. If he'd been more decisive, braver, maybe he'd still be with her.

Despite the emotional pain, he continues to breathe through the process. *I'm okay. I matter. This pain is important.*

Nolan closes his eyes tightly, continuing to acknowledge the emotional distress. It's uncomfortable. It's tense. But he keeps his focus on his emotional body and inhales deeply. As he exhales, all he can picture is Tori: how she'd stick out her tongue when she was thinking hard about something; how she'd sneeze three times in a row if she smelled even a hint of perfume; how she wasn't afraid to tell Nolan the truth.

Through the tears and heartache, Nolan can feel his heart warm. His love for her, though it will change and soften, will always be within him. And there was something incredibly comforting in that knowledge.

Nolan is able to take a deeper breath as his muscles relax. A sense of gratitude replaces the discomfort—gratitude for Tori pointing out Nolan's False Belonging Habit, thankfulness for the Crew teaching him how to Authentically Communicate, and pride for finally embracing his passions and trusting his decisions.

With his emotions in attunement, Nolan's Taho arises naturally, allowing him to walk through Door Three. He inhales and asks himself silently, *Where is my sense of love and value?*

Here, he responds in his mind, feeling the truth of the statement radiating from his chest.

Will turning down Uncle Leo's job change my love or value?

Nolan smiles and shakes his head. He turns around to look at himself in the mirror, now feeling confident in his choice. "You got this," he whispers, giving his reflection a high five before walking out of the bathroom.

Returning with a water and can of soda, Nolan asks Leo to talk privately for a moment.

"Sure thing," Leo says, winking at Nolan's dad as he stands up.

Under the shade of the towering tree, Nolan releases a breath and asks the key question of Authentic Communication: "Can I check in with you?"

"Uh, yeah, of course," Leo says, clearly a little thrown off by the question.

"Since you offered me the job, I've been stressed out. Like, *really* stressed," Nolan emphasizes.

"I get it," Leo chimes in. "It's a new industry. New group of guys to work with, but it's a solid job, Noli. I'll give you good benefits and plenty of time off..."

"I don't want to focus on the job right now, Uncle Leo. I want to tell you what's happening for me." As much as Leo wants to stay focused on the job, Nolan is determined to shift the focus to their connection. "When you offered me the job, I almost said yes, right away, because that's what I've always done—with my parents at least. It's like I just disappear into the background, doing whatever they want. It's awful, really." Nolan's voice breaks.

Nolan can see Leo swallow hard as he watches his nephew, but Nolan is no longer afraid of Leo's response. So, he continues on. "And you know what? I'm tired of it. I can't do the people-pleasing anymore." Nolan pauses, taking in a slow breath. "Instead, I want to listen to my gut. I want to trust myself! And actually, you offering me this job has helped me come face to face with that. I know I want to pursue my volunteer opportunity, no matter what else comes my way. So, thank you, for helping me realize that."

"Wow. I didn't know you were going through all that," Leo quietly replies. "Or else I wouldn't have offered you the job."

Again, Nolan is determined to stay focused on the connection. "You're not the only one. I've been playing a part for so long that no one knew, not even myself." Nolan straightened his back. "But I'm working on it. I've missed a lot being a people pleaser, so I'm trying to catch myself when I drift that way. I just wanted you to know how grateful I am for your support, and even for right now. *This*—being able to talk about it—is what's helping me change. So thank you for that too."

"Mmm," Leo says with a nod. "Would've been fun to have you in the office though." He seems to catch himself. "But never mind that—thanks for letting me know." He gives Nolan a small smile, then walks back to the rest of the family.

As Nolan stands alone, not an iota of shame or regret or self-consciousness plagues him. He feels a sense of freedom and a deep connection to himself, and to Leo. He's proud of staying true to himself, and he can feel his Taho radiating from within. Nolan takes a deep, calming breath, then rejoins his family with a shining grin.

Can you feel the triumph that Nolan is experiencing right now? This is what Authentic Communication offers us. When we share the experience of walking through the Three Doors with another person, the effects are multiplied.

Let's break down exactly how Nolan just Authentically Communicated. The first thing to note is that when we go through this process, we're no longer in a reactive state. Nolan was on the verge of being reactive when he first saw his uncle—but then he went through the Three Doors. He paused and observed, attuned to his emotions, and reconnected to his Taho. By the time Nolan rejoined Uncle Leo, he was past the reactive stage.

From this more balanced place, he could hone in on the three focuses of Authentic Communication—the first being zeroing in on the connection. Nolan started off by asking his uncle, "Can I check in with you?" to signal that connection was going to be the central point of the conversation. When we first Authentically Communicate with someone, we'll notice how often people will try to steer the conversation back to the original topic rather than the personal connection, because this is how most of us are taught to converse. Leo did this, didn't he? The check-in question surprised him, and he tried a few times to veer the conversation back to the topic of the job. However, Nolan was vigilant and kept steering the conversation back on course.

As he centered the conversation on connection, Nolan was already moving toward sharing emotionally, the second focus of Authentic Communication. First, he acknowledged his initial emotions by describing how stressed he was when Leo offered him the job. Then, he took it a level deeper by opening up about the pain of neglecting his own desires for so long.

As Nolan was sharing, those feelings all came back to the surface. By welcoming the emotions, Nolan stayed attuned to his emotional body. Through this attunement, Nolan was able to experience his Taho. Then, when he spoke about his ability to trust his decision, Nolan brought in the third focus of Authentic Communication: vocalizing your Taho. By *verbalizing* his innate value and love to another person, Nolan's Taho experienced yet another affirmation of recognition and acknowledgement. Nolan, staying in connection, then thanked his uncle for talking with him.

Uncle Leo didn't respond poorly, but he also didn't dive into sharing in earnest himself. This highlights a major aspect of

Authentic Communication: the other person's response does not determine our experience. Regardless of the reply, we can feel that we've moved closer to ourselves because *we* were real. We've gotten to the source of our own distress and, in doing so, reclaimed our connection with our innermost wholeness. And by expressing ourselves in a real way, we can feel closer to the person, no matter how they respond. We know full well that we are now far more connected with them than we would have been had we reacted with an emotional explosion or implosion.

Authentically communicating nudges us to trust vulnerability again and again. We shift out of feelings of insecurity and fear of rejection, and we move into conversations grounded in our own integrity.

When we choose to integrate the three focuses of Authentic Communication—zeroing in on connection, sharing our emotional experiences, and vocalizing our Taho—into our lives, opportunities for unrestricted connection show up everywhere. Let's see how you can begin to create these authentic conversations in your own life.

ADOPTING AUTHENTIC COMMUNICATION

Now that you've seen how Nolan navigated Authentic Communication, let's flesh out what it would look like for you to do this. Imagine, right now, someone close to you says, "Whoa, you spent that much money?!" Notice the feeling. Let's picture what it would look like to move through the Three Doors and then share that experience through Authentic Communication.

Door One: Pausing Your Conditioned Thoughts

Right after hearing that comment, your inner monologue may be sounding off with thoughts like: *Why are they telling me how to spend my money? They should mind their own business!*

Once you notice the specific, familiar tone of these thoughts, that's your signal to take a deep breath. Quickly imagine what would transpire if you responded with a defensive, knee-jerk reaction. You might start a debate about who's right or criticize them for a recent purchase of their own.

This is Door One. Visualize the amount of disconnection that will take place if you follow these defensive thoughts. Become aware of what will happen to your connection with yourself and with the other person if you blow a gasket.

Excuse yourself for a moment as you take a pause. As you begin facing uncomfortable feelings, dig into your courage.

Door Two: Attuning to Your Emotional Body

For many of us, it can be difficult to descend into our emotional body because our mind is still occupied with complaints about the other person. We feel like we need to defend ourselves. In truth, though, we're trying to protect our tender underbelly, the innate love and value that is our core (which we unconsciously believe is being threatened).

When we're in a reactive mode, it's hard to see that we're being defensive. So, we meet ourselves where we're at. We use our reactivity to our advantage—by *mindfully* replaying our judgments about the other person. *Who are they to tell me what to do? They think they know better than me.*

Rather than getting sucked into this narrative, we shift our focus to welcoming the emotion that accompanies these thoughts. What do you feel when you observe these judgments? Annoyance? Dejection? Remind yourself that this feeling is valid and important.

Once you're fully experiencing this initial emotion, it's time to go a step deeper. Turn these critiques toward yourself (and remove any judgment about the other person). *They do know better than me. I'm so stupid.*

Can you feel the anxiety that's coming up? Allow this feeling of anxiety to intensify. How does it feel to have this self-damning voice in your head? Now shift your attention from those judgmental thoughts and give your entire focus to the anxiety. Feel the nuances. Feel the dread of rejection. Feel the fear of making the wrong decision. As you experience these anxious feelings, you're getting closer to the real source of your distress.

Continue to tell yourself that what you're experiencing is okay. Make the time and space to feel this. Breathe. Accept anything and everything that's coming up for you. Keep reminding yourself, "It's okay for me to feel this way. These emotions are valid." You can even try speaking directly to your emotional body, saying "I won't abandon you. You deserve to be seen. I'm here for you." This unconditional acceptance of your formerly rejected feelings is what soothes you.

Inhale a deep, chest-expanding breath.

Exhale and feel your shoulders relax.

Do you feel a need to keep justifying the money you spent? This is your False Belonging Habit trying to butt in. Keep allowing and honoring your emotions. Breathe, observe, and honor the process.

Allow yourself to experience the full weight of thinking you need to make the "right" choice. Feel the tension of believing that you have to follow someone else's idea of what you should do and be. Can you feel this discomfort in your body? Can you feel the cost of trying to live up to others' standards?

Don't rush. Experience this symphony of emotions with an open and forgiving heart. The more you acknowledge them, the more your emotional body will feel seen.

You might find that your focus and calm presence will begin to soothe you more and more. This moment of peace is the sign that you have re-established the connection with your innate love and value at the body level.

Door Three: Affirming Your Taho

Take the time and assess your connection with your emotional body. If you still find yourself wanting to react, continue to attune and make space for your emotions. Remember, sometimes your mind will want to skip straight to the end. If you hang in there until you've fully attuned to yourself, calm centeredness will happen naturally.

Once you feel your breath loosen up and your internal angst lessening, dig deep and ask yourself, "Where is my love and value?" In your body, here and now, where is your sense of love and value? Did you lose it from spending that money? Or is your wholeness, your Taho, right where it's always been?

Authentically Communicate

Once you've reconnected with your Taho, you can go back to the other person and ask, "Can I check in with you?" With this question, you're inviting the person to join you in authentically communicating.

Stick to the three focuses of Authentic Communication as you resume the conversation. Throughout the interaction, you can continue to steer the conversation away from the topic and toward connection. Even if the other person keeps repeating the topic (the money), stay laser-focused on the person-to-person connection above all else.

Now, highlight the second focus of Authentic Communication by sharing your emotional experience. First, you might reassure the person by saying, "I want you to know I'm not blaming you for my feelings. I had an intense reaction." Then, sharing your feelings could look like: "I noticed after you made that comment, I started feeling really anxious. I questioned if I made the right decision. I felt stupid."

Take a moment and breathe. Notice how you're not reacting or fueling a story. Attuning to your emotional body has allowed you to simply report what you experienced, without judgment.

Notice what it feels like to be vulnerable and to have your emotions witnessed. Feel that in your body. Stay with that feeling of authenticity.

Once you're aware of how you're no longer putting your innate love or value in question, speak to that experience. "Isn't it amazing what I put myself through sometimes? I'm not stupid. I know that."

Take a moment to feel how you've just vocalized your connection to your Taho. That's what matters. Your connection is strong.

Regardless of the other person's response, the most important thing is that you shared your authentic truth. You're connected to your Taho, your innermost self. From this place, you can choose what to do next. You can ask for some space. You can ask to continue the conversation around the money later.

Whatever route you choose, take a moment to express your appreciation by saying something like, "I'm grateful that I had this opportunity to share my experience with you." Can you feel how you're truly prioritizing connection with your Taho and with the other person?

Choosing to be vulnerable with another person can be a game changer. Authentic Communication allows you to be valued for who you and to cultivate connection.

EASING INTO AUTHENTIC COMMUNICATION

Authentic Communication requires patience, practice, and commitment, so don't jump into it in every environment with every single person you meet. After all, a meeting at work might get a tad uncomfortable if you decide to get vulnerable during a financing pitch. Read the room, and read your own readiness.

As you prepare to embrace Authentic Communication in your life, there are some steps you can take to help ease you into this way of life.

Start with your safe person

To start integrating your commitment to authenticity, it's helpful to find one trusted person with whom you feel safe (or nearly safe!) being vulnerable. You can work out the kinks by using this communication style with this confidante. Voice your thoughts, reveal your feelings, and build confidence in speaking this openly. It's a wonderful opportunity to experience how powerful it feels when someone else is able to hear you voice your truths.

Sharing is your choice

Authentic Communication is not "all or nothing." Just because you decide to speak what's true for you doesn't mean you have to bare every inch of your soul. *You* get to decide how many details you want to share, and that amount may ebb and flow depending on the situation, and on who you are communicating with.

Trust that you know what to share. This is not about airing dirty laundry or abandoning discernment. It's about a kind of communication that is mindful and honoring. Connection is sacred—treat it that way.

Choosing not to share can also be self-care

Sometimes we need to be alone with our thoughts before we talk about them. In moments like this, we can recognize that Authentic Communication isn't what we need right now.

For example, after Rowan learned of his mother's terminal illness, did he immediately try to talk to her about it? No. They were both quiet as they felt the ground shift beneath them. They needed time to feel the monumental change happening in their lives.

Take time for yourself. Listen. Bless your own timing.

Make space for change and connection to grow

Our loved ones are used to us behaving in a certain way. You have them pegged too, right? So, it will take some time for them to expect Authentic Communication instead of arguments or stone-walling. It will take time for the dynamics to change. That's okay. Breathe.

When Tate and Molly got back together, Molly was always waiting for Tate to get upset when she'd buy something or when the credit card bill came in. That's what she'd been used to for the past fifteen years of their marriage, after all. Yet, Tate began to respond in a different way. He was calm and open. Tate kept communicating authentically—ten, twenty, thirty times. Over time, Molly slowly changed what she anticipated from Tate.

This is the same for our own family and friends. As they see us changing, their expectations will start changing too. Oftentimes, their own walls will start to come down as they see how we've cultivated a safer and more authentic environment. After all, isn't that what we all crave?

Take time to savor the feeling of connection

After you authentically communicate, take a moment to savor the experience in your body. Notice how it feels to lower your walls, and to be so real. How does your body feel when you are vulnerable despite the fear and the risk? It's a freeing feeling, isn't it?

Don't rush past this feeling.

When you take a moment to bathe in this experience, it leaves a mark. That warm connection settles into the body's memory. Then, the next time you're feeling nervous about being open, you can take a moment to breathe and connect back to this memory. To remember the freeing feeling. To remember how the weight of anxiety lifted off your chest. To remember the power of validating your true belonging with a trusted person in your life.

You can be open. You are so beautiful when you are authentic. You deserve to be seen, valued, and loved for who you truly are.

CHAPTER 14

CREATING EXPERIENCES OF BELONGING

We all have this ability, as we've seen, to authentically connect, attune, and make a safe space. When we focus on connection, it becomes second nature, and we see opportunities for authenticity everywhere.

Imagine that you run into an acquaintance from your last job. You ask how her boyfriend is doing and she looks down, saying, "Actually, we just broke up."

In the past, you may have reacted to this situation by apologizing for bringing it up or changing the topic. Now, our new instinct is to attune to this person and ask, "What's that been like for you?"

Connection instead of nervous self-doubt. Connection instead of insecurity and self-absorption. Connection instead of that long-held habit of correction and fixing. Wow, what a shift we've made!

As we tap into our Taho, reclaiming our true belonging, an amazing realization occurs. We can see that we don't need to correct or change ourselves. We are no longer devout to our False

Belonging Habits. We are feeling, deep in our bones, that we already have everything we need to truly belong.

Connection is our natural state of being. We humans reach our potential through the bonds we forge and the relationships we nurture and build. As we prioritize connection, we naturally fall into rhythm, just like the Crew has. Over and over, they choose to prioritize connection. You can do the same, because you are the very essence of courage, resilience, inherent value, and love.

Take a deep breath and close your eyes, allowing yourself to feel these truths within you.

Through connection, we find purpose, acceptance, and love.

Through connection, we belong.

BELONGING IN COMMUNITY

Once practicing the Three Doors and the three focuses of Authentic Communication becomes a consistent part of our lives, a natural progression happens.

First, our self-acceptance increases. We reconnect with our Taho, release our False Belonging Habits, and no longer waste energy trying to belong in surface-level ways. We become more confident in who we are—strengths, shortcomings, and all. We feel safe being authentic with others.

As we feel more secure in authentically communicating with those in our life, another shift can take place. Now, rather than just sharing our own emotional experiences, we'll want to actively boost up others. We'll feel the desire to contribute.

When we think of contributing, we tend to think of two of the most common forms: financial contribution (donating money) and physical contribution (volunteering). These are both very needed and very necessary. Yet, there is another form of contributing that is equally needed, but desperately lacking, in our world: connection-based contribution.

To understand this kind of contribution, think back to when Callie and Liam stopped by The Hearth for a sweet treat. Rowan could have come out, said hello, and bid them farewell, but he had seen how Callie was hurting, and he knew she would benefit from a safe space to open up. So, he invited her on a hike with the rest of the Crew. And what did Callie discover in this group of people? Complete acceptance. She could finally be herself and express her feelings without feeling judged.

The Crew creating that safe space for Callie is precisely what we mean by connection-based contribution.

It's no surprise that Rowan is an expert in this kind of gifting.

His mother understood the beautiful flow of giving and receiving, and she taught Rowan how to strike this balance from a young age. And this is what he did for the Crew.

Rowan created safe places for each Crew member to be able to share authentically, shed their False Belonging Habits, and eventually reconnect with their Taho.

He did this with Kenta, by inviting him to flourish while engaging in his passion.

He did this with Amani, by helping her receive nurturance in this community.

He did this with Mia, by showing her love and acceptance at work and at play from a young age.

He did this with Tate, by lovingly challenging his anxiety.

He did this with Callie, validating her feelings by sharing his own emotions.

And he did this with Nolan, by showing him his worthiness.

Yet, it wasn't just Rowan who contributed. After being around him, the Crew began to contribute in many different ways. They offered to clean Nolan's apartment. They volunteered for Rowan's mother's fundraiser without hesitation. Over and over, they offered connection-based contributions.

Kenta encouraged Amani to let in the feeling of being pampered at The Hearth.

Tate and Amani supported Callie on the hike after she tried to shut down her emotions.

Mia acknowledged what a multilayered and creative person Nolan is when he wasn't yet able to see it himself.

After they were each able to tap into their own innate wholeness, the Crew wanted to help others experience *their* Taho. This formed the foundation of their open and authentic little community. Where self-acceptance, connection, and contribution meet—this is where the most vibrant experience of belonging lives. When we can truly honor ourselves, and safely communicate and connect, we celebrate the deep and brilliant value and love that we each possess.

This is the community that Rowan's mother envisioned.

This is what it means to live a life of Avive la Vie.

AN INVITATION TO JOIN AVIVE LA VIE

Avive la Vie—An Adventure in Belonging is a community designed to support you on your journey. It is a hub for connection, using in-person weekend adventures and online groups to help you begin to experience a sense of true belonging.

It is my dream that we—all people, throughout the world—will experience the deep nurturing of connection. It has been so exciting to see how people have related to each other's sharing and have deeply connected with their own innate love and value. As we work together to build belonging, we grow our strength, our radiance, our aliveness! We welcome you to take the first big step and join us. We invite you, with your wonderful uniqueness, to bring your special insights. You already belong.

www.avivelavie.com
J.F. Benoist

ACKNOWLEDGMENTS

I couldn't have completed this book without the love and support of some extraordinary people.

To my wife, Joyce, thank you for your endless patience, encouragement, and belief in me—you are my rock forever.

Thank you to my mother, Micheline Sauriol. You have provided unwavering support and wisdom and guided me through every chapter of my life.

Mark Watson, who blessed me with honest feedback and constant encouragement. I'm grateful for your insights and always being there for me.

I want to express my heartfelt thanks to my editors, Emily Pogue, David Cates, Brooke Carey, and Danielle Anderson. Your guidance has been invaluable.

And to all my clients, participants, and especially my first cohort of Avive la Vie. You have inspired me and are a testament to human strength and heroism. Thank you from the bottom of my heart.

ABOUT THE AUTHOR

Jean-Francois (J.F.) Benoist is a mental health pioneer and the author of the best-selling self-help book *Addicted to the Monkey Mind*. For over a decade, he and his wife Joyce operated a cutting-edge holistic addiction treatment center in Hawaii.

Benoist is the founder of the Avive la Vie Organization and a Certified Option Process Mentor/Counselor. He also serves as an international leader emeritus for The Mankind Project, a nonprofit organization focused on supporting and training men to live with integrity. He is the creator of the therapeutic methodology Experiential Engagement Therapy™ (EET), which focuses on addressing underlying core beliefs. He is known for his authentic, experiential techniques that maximize long-term change.

After decades of working with people, J.F. observed how a lack of connection and sense of belonging profoundly affects a person's ability to access their true nature. This life-changing work led him to launch the Avive la Vie movement and write the book *Avive la*

Vie—An Adventure in Belonging. The powerful work of Avive la Vie can be found at Benoist's podcast, workshops, professional trainings, and speaking engagements.

To find more information about J.F. Benoist and the Avive la Vie programs, please visit the following websites:

YouTube: @Avivelavie
www.AviveLaVie.com
www.JFBenoist.com

ENJOYED YOUR JOURNEY WITH US?

We hope you found *Avive la Vie* enlightening and engaging. If you have a moment, **please consider leaving a review on Amazon or Goodreads.** Your feedback not only helps us spread the word, but also assists fellow readers in discovering books they might love.

We sincerely appreciate your support and hope that this work brings you joy. Thank you for being a part of the Avive la Vie journey!

Amazon Review

Goodreads Review

Made in United States
Troutdale, OR
02/01/2025

28479838R00146